FACILITATING COMMUNITY CHANGE:
A BASIC GUIDE

FACILITATING COMMUNITY CHANGE

A Basic Guide

by

Donald R. Fessler

University Associates, Inc.
8517 Production Avenue
P.O. Box 26240
San Diego, California 92126

FOREWORD

This book is intended for two types of individuals:

1) the specialist in any one of a number of technical fields who finds himself inadequately prepared for the major responsibility of working with people to bring about change at the community level;

2) the concerned private citizen who finds that his efforts to involve others in finding solutions to the many community problems they face have been unproductive for lack of broad support.

The first we can call the professional and the latter the nonprofessional change agent.

The book draws on some long-accepted concepts in the field of group process as well as first-hand experience in organizing change efforts at the community, county, and multicounty level.

The major assumption of this book is that before changes can be brought about to solve community problems, a much larger and more representative number of citizens will need to be involved in the decision-making process. For citizens to do the job effectively, they will need an understanding of group process and a command of its skills— capabilities which are acquired through training and practice. The aspiring change agent needs to provide them with such training if they are to meet their responsibilities. For this reason the chapters near the end of the book have been designed as a workshop manual which can be used both for this purpose and to arouse interest in bringing about change through cooperative community effort.

In fact, the book is organized on a principle of increasing specificity. The first five chapters describe the general climate and community conditions within which the professional change agent must work. Succeeding chapters deal with the day-to-day problems he will face and suggest principles and practices for dealing with them.

The REFERENCES AND READINGS at the end of each chapter have been chosen with two purposes in mind: first, to help the reader recognize that the theoretical ideas presented in each chapter are based on scientifically controlled experiments or on operational research by social scientists of recognized standing, and, second, to familiarize readers with some of the literature in the field that can enhance their ability to work with people in planning change.

Donald R. Fessler
Blacksburg, Virginia
June, 1976

TABLE OF CONTENTS

1

CHANGE AND THE SOCIAL ENVIRONMENT

ROADBLOCKS TO CHANGE EFFORTS

Social and technological changes have taken place in American society at a faster pace during our lifetime than at any other time in recorded history. However, attempts at national, state, and local levels to bring such changes under control, while increasing in number, have not been markedly successful in recent years. In fact the crisis proportions of problems such as environmental pollution, energy depletion, and rising crime rates indicate that we are failing to achieve changes that might be beneficial to us and our cherished way of life.

More than a century ago de Tocqueville noted that Americans had a unique flair for organizing themselves into groups to deal with problems. We seem not to have lost this organizing fervor, judging by the proliferation of organizations, agencies, and ad hoc groups dealing with every known problem under the sun. We are not, however, getting results commensurate with the effort expended or the gravity of the problems.

There are a number of reasons for our growing inability to control change. The first is undoubtedly the tremendous increase in our population and its concentration in urban areas. While higher literacy rates and the availability of mass media such as radio, television, and the press make superficial communication easier than ever before, the increasing depersonalization of human relationships has reduced real communication. Without the genuine sharing of concerns and aspirations by the general population, planned change geared to the needs of all seldom takes place or, more often than not, it falls short of full implementation.

The second reason is the growth of government bureaucracy. In an earlier day, when educated people were a small proportion of a predom-

1

inantly agricultural population, the need for technical guidance was overwhelming, and the people rightly turned to government for help. Government assistance was an important ingredient in our nation's economic development. In recent years, however, the educational level of people in both rural and urban areas has risen and most of them are quite capable of working out solutions to their problems themselves or are able to pay for the help they need. Yet government agencies keep on growing from year to year. Where they recruit volunteer support, they divert the efforts of community leaders from solving community problems to perpetuating the programs of their sponsoring agencies.

The third reason is closely related to the second. Americans have become persuaded that technology can solve all their problems. Even though the problems they face are likely to be people problems rather than technical problems, they let professionally trained technicians make decisions for them that they ought to be making for themselves. Most government bureaucracies are dominated by experts in various technical fields. Agency programs are built around the technical aspects of general community problems rather than the process by which the people in each community reach agreement on what their problems are and what they want to do about them.

Fourth, as a result of the propensity that de Tocqueville alluded to, a great many organizations, agencies, and committees—official and otherwise—are dedicated to making their communities better places in which to live. Each attempts on its own to do something about the more glaring problems and there is usually considerable duplication of effort and, at best, only piecemeal results. As a result, human resources are dissipated and organizational barriers get in the way of coordinated community effort.

Finally, we must recognize that government itself is a major factor both in bringing about change and in frustrating change efforts. It would be foolish to ignore the dominating power of moneyed interests over all branches of our government at the federal, state, and local levels. As long as elected officials and representatives need huge sums of money to achieve and retain office, this power will not be diminished. Hence government measures too frequently favor the influential and leave the original problem unsolved. To overcome this, people must voluntarily organize to make known, and get, the kinds of living conditions they would prefer. They, not the officials or bureaucrats, ought to dominate the process of planned change.

All this means is that, in the process of planned change in America at present, decisions are made "for" people rather than "by" them, and a large proportion of changes benefit a privileged sector of society only and leave many new and often more serious problems in their wake. Planning decisions that might benefit the people as a whole are not implemented because citizens are not sufficiently involved in the decision-making process to recognize their value and rally to their support.

THE VARIETIES OF PLANNED CHANGE

At this point we need to distinguish between two kinds or levels of change efforts. The first includes attempts by formal and informal organizations, government agencies, and community groups to change the attitudes and practices of individual citizens in either their private or their professional capacities. Presumably these changes will be in the interest of the community at large. Many of these objectives are established at the state or national level and may constitute a major proportion of an agency's activities. Programs to update farm and forestry practices, to improve home management, child care, physical and mental health, and nutrition are of this type. Occasionally such change efforts are initiated by local groups.

The success of these change efforts is best measured by the number of individuals who adopt the recommended attitudes or practices. Individual involvement is imperative. Unfortunately, agencies or private organizations that initiate changes of this kind tend to develop across-the-board programs which may not satisfy what local people see as their needs. Programs to control Bang's disease, for example, have been promoted by agricultural specialists in farm areas where few cows are kept for dairy pruposes. To the agencies, 100 percent area-wide participation in their pet programs is more important than solving the problems of individual communities.

The second kind of planned change effort consists of those organized, cooperative efforts to improve the institutional operations and facilities of a community in order to help overcome community-wide problems. They include such community development efforts as bringing in industry, upgrading community recreational programs for young people, and creating better employment opportunities for local citizens. These efforts at change are largely project-oriented, although some government agencies as well as private organizations (the U.S. Chamber of Commerce, for example) have undertaken to develop program formulas for dealing with them. The success of these projects can be measured not only by the extent to which specific objectives are achieved, but probably even more importantly by the degree to which all community-minded organizations have participated in the change effort. The development of a cooperative spirit among local groups for the purpose of dealing with common problems can be much more valuable to the ongoing life of the community than the accomplishment of any particular agreed-upon goal.

TECHNOLOGY AND CHANGE

Many of the more serious problems in the United States, such as the deterioration of the natural environment, are due to the uncontrolled use of technological advances to satisfy the profit- and power-hungry demands of limited segments of the population. Because of this situation, there has grown up (especially among young people) a strong resistance to technology as such and a desire to turn back to less-complex ways of living.

This attitude toward technology can have serious consequences, particularly at the local level. Technology is basically the application of science to the production and distribution of goods to satisfy man's needs. As world populations increase, so do the demands for more food, clothing, and shelter, and the simple production and distribution techniques of an earlier day prove increasingly inadequate. Unless technology keeps pace with population, millions will be condemned to starvation, exposure and death. No one can justifiably exempt himself from sharing the burdens of a growing technology. New ways of determining and enforcing the wishes of the people must be devised and effectively utilized, not to eliminate technology, but to insure that it is used for the benefit of all.

THE CASE FOR PLANNED CHANGE

The effects of technology on our natural environment, the excessive demands made on our physical resources by our growing affluence and our growing population, the deprivation of basic human needs for a shockingly large proportion of people—all have created problems that demand the utmost technical and social skills to resolve. These problems will not solve themselves. If they are not faced, they will spawn other problems which can in time envelop and destroy our society.

But many who have tried to come to grips with these problems have found that they have only made matters worse, have started something they could not finish for lack of popular support, or have run into insurmountable opposition. Despite the best of intentions something has been wrong with their approach. The obstacles they have encountered have their origin in the structure of society and in an ignorance of the dynamics of effective group action.

REFERENCES AND READINGS

Cartwright, D., & Zander, A. (Eds.). *Group dynamics: Research and theory* (3rd ed.). New York: Harper & Row, 1968.

Drucker, P. *Technology, management and society*. New York: Harper & Row, 1970.

Fischer, J. *Vital signs: U.S.A.* New York: Harper & Row, 1975.

Friedmann, J. *Retracking America*. Garden City, N.Y.: Anchor/Doubleday, 1973.

Hoffer, E. Drastic change. In D. P. Lauda & R. D. Ryan (Eds.), *Advancing technology: Its impact on society*. Dubuque, Iowa: Wm. C. Brown, 1971.

Kranzberg, M., & Pursell, C. W., Jr. The importance of technology in human affairs. In D. P. Lauda & R. D. Ryan (Eds.), *Advancing technology: Its impact on society*. Dubuque, Iowa: Wm. C. Brown, 1971.

Warren, R. Types of purposive change at the community level. In R. Kramer & H. Specht (Eds.), *Readings in community organization practice*. Englewood Cliffs, N.J.: Prentice-Hall, 1969.

2

SOME SOCIOLOGICAL FACTORS IN CHANGE

In light of the barriers to planned change, it is important to identify some of the sociological factors in the environment in which organized change efforts are expected to operate.

THE SENSE OF COMMUNITY

In this context the term *community* comes readily to mind. If community is defined, however, as sociologists define it, as any area in which people with a common culture share common interests, it will be much too flexible for the purpose. The term could obviously be applied to a rural village of half a hundred families and at the same time to a large metropolitan area such as any one of our major cities. These latter, as we know, are generally characterized by that depersonalization of human relationships that makes cooperative efforts to deal with common problems difficult in the extreme.

Community, then, to be a suitable locus for change efforts, must have a sufficient degree of primariness to make genuine interpersonal communication possible. That is, the people who associate in change efforts, even if only for the first time, must have sufficient knowledge or awareness of the backgrounds of their new associates to be able to relate to them in a meaningful manner. This is rarely possible when people are drawn from areas so far from one another geographically and socially that they have little concept of how the others live or think. To be sure, this handicap can be overcome when people meet together for extended periods of time in conferences and retreats. But in most change programs that deal with community rather than personal problems, these extended contacts are rare.

Furthermore, because of certain variables, there is no way to set standards of primariness that will fit all communities. These variables include the age of the community, the rigidity of its class structure, the size and nature of its geographical setting, and very importantly, the degree of mobility of the people in and out of the area. Where a sufficient degree of primariness does exist, however, there will be that sense of community that is essential to cooperative action, and this often can be determined by a spot check of the citizens themselves. Generally speaking, if they express a "feel" for the community as such, that may prove sufficient.

In most newly formed multicounty planning or development districts, whether predominantly rural or urban or a combination of both, there will be little sense of community for the district as a whole unless unique historical or geographical factors have existed over a fairly long period of time and mobility in and out of the area has been low. In most planning districts, then, attempts at planned change are best initiated at a lower level, preferably the county, in hopes that in time the very planning process itself will help to build the district-wide sense of community that is desired. When the individual counties in a district have identified their respective problems and these are seen to be more or less the same, the problems can be consolidated and the efforts of the problem-solving groups can be coordinated. Educational programs, for example, to inform people of the merits and limitations of available alternatives, may often be prepared at the district level for use by counties. And whenever this process of consolidation can bring the county problem-solving groups together at the district level, the individuals involved will begin to recognize the interests and concerns they have in common, and a sense of community will begin to develop. As solutions to common problems are reached, this sense of community will be shared by the organizations the members of the problem-solving groups belong to, and from them it will be extended to the general population.

In metropolitan areas where little sense of community exists, the separate inner-city and suburban political jurisdictions can be dealt with in a similar fashion. Neighborhood problems and concerns can gradually be consolidated into metropolis-wide programs that may develop a highly desirable sense of community instrumental in resolving future problems.

INSTITUTIONAL FRAMEWORK OF CHANGE EFFORTS

The activities that people carry on in the course of their day-to-day existence fall into certain patterns, referred to as the institutions of society. They are often defined by social scientists as the established forms and procedures characteristic of group activity. They make it possible to distinguish among those aspects of our lives that are familial, economic, religious, educational, political, and so on.

Within these institutions there are organizations and associations such as banks, churches, hospitals, schools, and agencies of government which enable people cooperatively to achieve the institutional goals expected of them.

Problems or needs that arise at the community level are frequently perceived first by the members of one of these organizations because the problems have a direct impact on the activities of the institution that the organization is a part of and to some degree controls. Whenever this happens, the organization may take the responsibility for finding solutions.

However, the causes of community problems can seldom be neatly generalized and laid at the door of any one institution in society. They involve factors stemming from many institutions. The failure of some people, for example, to acquire the skills they need to become well-adjusted members of society may not be due at all to failings in the schools, but stem from family situations or unidentified physical or mental handicaps.

When the attempt to solve community problems is dominated by institutionally related organizations or agencies, it frequently happens that the aspects of the problem being considered and the solutions recommended fit too neatly into an institutional pattern and miss completely the real problem at hand. At best the "solutions" will be only mitigating and will cause more serious problems in the future. The handling of the race problem primarily through the schools is a case in point.

Genuine solutions to community problems are more likely to be achieved when representatives of all aspects of community life are involved in the problem-solving endeavors. Only then will real problems, rather than the symptoms of problems, be identified and the solutions be to the credit and benefit of the whole community rather than the separate organizations or agencies within it.

THE DECLINE OF MIDDLE-CLASS DOMINANCE OF COMMUNITY NORMS

American society has often been referred to as a middle-class society, one in which the norms accepted by a majority of the people are largely determined by those who have achieved certain economic, social, and educational standards. These norms, developed out of long experience, are assumed to be the best means for achieving institutional objectives for the community and its individual members. While many of these norms still have validity, some have begun to lose their relevance as the nation has moved from a predominantly agrarian to an urban, industrial society, and still others are hotly debated at the present time.

At the turn of the century, and again during the Great Depression, many members of the lower classes found it impossible to maintain middle-class norms in their day-to-day activities even when they desperately desired to do so. Their families were not always able to keep their children in school and to clothe and feed them properly, and they were unable to provide proper care for the sick and the elderly. But in those days these families did not count, either socially or politically, in the total scheme of things and their deviance from the norms did not matter.

During World War I, and even more so in World War II, in the armed forces and in industry, many members of the economically depressed classes were, for the first time, brought into touch, more or less as equals, with members of the middle class and became aware of the benefits enjoyed by the latter which they did not share. As they fought and labored for their country, they could not see why they should be excluded from enjoying these same benefits of an affluent society even if as individuals they were not always able to pay for them. They used their rights as voters to make their grievances known. As the power of these disadvantaged groups became manifest at the polls, astute politicians took up their cause and helped them secure these benefits through an expanding number of government programs.

In a democracy, then, as the electorate broadens, benefits that were previously thought to be the prerogative of the upper and middle classes are extended to all, old institutional attitudes and practices break down, and even in the middle class the old norms no longer carry the weight they once did. In fact, a reciprocal process often takes place, and norms once thought to be characteristic of certain disadvantaged groups are accepted by the society as a whole.

If old institutional norms give way and agreement is not reached on what new norms should take their place, anarchy can prevail and destroy a society. But the middle class by itself no longer can have the exclusive right to determine what the new norms should be, if these norms are to be effective. The people as a whole must be involved in deciding what new norms are best in all their institutional activities. This effort is what planned change is all about.

INSTITUTIONAL RESISTANCE TO CHANGE

Those who undertake to bring about change in an orderly fashion will often be discouraged by the high degree of resistance to change that they find among the people with whom they are trying to work. They will be doubly discouraged by the fact that the strongest resistance often comes from those who occupy official positions in the institutional framework of society.

This rigidity of institutions provides people with a sense of stability they would not otherwise have, but when carried too far it can prevent institutions from meeting the human needs they were intended to serve. Social scientists have pointed out several reasons for this rigidity.

Within each social institution, people join together in associations and organizations to cooperate in achieving mutual goals. Such associations are organized to survive, and to their paid personnel and advisory boards, they can become ends in themselves rather than a means of satisfying human needs. How different today, for example, are our major denominational bodies from the loose-knit groups of earnest seekers after truth who gathered beside the Sea of Galilee.

In order to strengthen their ability to survive, these organizations create regulations and ideologies which in time become absolutes and from which deviations are not permitted. To enforce the regulations, more and more authority is concentrated at the top. To save both time and effort, administrators follow set routines, hold to the path of least resistance, and operate through chains of command that effectively shield them from those who disagree with them. These chains of command are generally built on seniority, that is, on those who have proven through long service that they are loyal to established procedures. Needless paperwork and endless consultations are substituted for action, and in this way the changing needs of the people the institutions are supposed to serve are ignored.

Eventually most of these organizations become inflexible bureaucracies whose complex procedures impede action while providing the appearance of purposeful activity. Promotion is not based on how well staff members help to solve human problems, but on how well they publicize the organization, how much they publish, how many government or foundation grants they obtain, and how completely they subordinate themselves to the organization, that is, to the wishes of those above them in the chain of command.

An enterprising social scientist (Downs, 1967) formulated some laws related to the size of such organizations and their ability to make the decisions needed to cope with social change. According to these laws, the larger the organization, the weaker the control of those at the top over its actions and the poorer the coordination of its actions. These limitations are attributed primarily to the fact that the vision of the decision makers at the top is limited, but it must also be recognized that the larger the organization, the more diverse are the internal and external pressures on the decision makers. A government agency, for example, has to take into account the demands of its particular client system, the wishes of the politicians who control its budget, the voters who elect the politicians, and the needs of its own operating personnel. These concerns become more diverse as the size of the organization increases and the scope of its operations broadens. They make decision making more and more complicated and encourage compromises that, more often than not, fall short of providing satisfactory solutions to the problems at hand.

Voluntary organizations are no less subject to these bureaucratic characteristics. The more successful they become, the more their success becomes a factor in their rigidity. They acquire professional staffs that have a vested interest in the survival of the organization and much less concern for solving the problems their associations were organized to deal with. For example, how many community health councils, once they were funded and staffed, have added to, rather than diminished, the obstacles to coordinating local health activities?

Within all institutions of society, personal conduct and social relations are tested by the dictates of precedence rather than experimentation. Moral codes established more than two thousand years ago in a pastoral society are still expected to be relevant to a highly urbanized, technological society. Since the organizations within various institutions assume the responsibility of maintaining the rules of conduct and procedure inherited from the past, the more the official representatives of these organizations dominate community decision making, the more insistence there will be to "go by the book" and avoid new and untried ways of solving age-old problems.[1]

BASIC GUIDELINES FOR COMMUNITY CHANGE

With these characteristics of social institutions in mind, we can arrive at some basic guidelines that should be helpful in bringing about change and in dealing with community problems.

First, attempts at planned change should be initiated at that level of community where people have a sufficient degree of primariness to

---

[1] To make the point, which I think is crucial, that much of the present resistance to change is due to bureaucratic inflexibility, I have drawn heavily on J. O. Hertzler's classic, *Social Institutions (1946)*, for this analysis.

make genuine interpersonal communication possible. In multicounty planning districts this means beginning with the separate county units, and in large metropolitan centers, the suburban and inner-city political jurisdictions.

Second, the more that community problems can be dealt with across institutional lines, free of the domination of any one institution, the greater will be the chances of breaking away from the limitations of the past and arriving at workable solutions that are in the interest of the total community.

Third, the more that concerned citizens outnumber bureaucrats in the decision-making process, the greater will be the possibility of putting the needs of the people above the survival of the bureaucracies.

And finally, to the extent that contemplated change will necessitate establishing new norms of thought and behavior for the community as a whole, it is essential that citizens representing organizations from all socioeconomic levels be included in the decision making.

REFERENCES AND READINGS

Benne, K. D. Democratic ethics and human engineering. In W. G. Bennis, K. D. Benne & R. Chin (Eds.), *The planning of change*. New York: Holt, Rinehart & Winston, 1962.

Biddle, W. W., & Biddle, L. J. *The community development process*. New York: Holt, Rinehart & Winston, 1965.

Downs, A. *Inside bureaucracy*. Boston: Little, Brown & Co., 1967.

Goodenough, W. H. Problems of practice: The agent. In *Cooperation in change*. New York: Russell Sage Foundation, 1963.

Hertzler, J. O. *Social Institutions*. Lincoln, Neb.: University of Nebraska Press, 1946.

Nisbet, R. *Social change*. Oxford: Basil Blackwell, 1972.

3

INVOLVING THE DISADVANTAGED
AND THE UNINTERESTED IN CHANGE

THE CONTINUUM OF MAJORITY
AND DISADVANTAGED CULTURES

Many community problems relate to the needs of low-income families and people on welfare. Their housing, their health, their recreation needs, and their schooling all make demands on community institutions different from those of the more affluent classes. If genuine solutions are to be found for the problems that affect them, these people will have to be involved in planning change. But achieving this involvement can be difficult.

As a class these people can be called disadvantaged in comparison with the citizens who constitute the majority culture. They lack the skills, the opportunities, or the motivation to enjoy a satisfactory life in a technological society. For the most part they are the victims of circumstances over which they have little or no control. If they are to participate in efforts toward change, their needs must be better understood.

A combination of circumstances occasionally makes it possible for members of this class to overcome their handicaps, become upwardly mobile, and, in time, identify themselves with the majority culture. Unusual employment opportunities for unskilled labor during World War II, for example, made this possible for hundreds of men and women who had previously known only a subsistence-level existence.

When this happens, these individuals may take on some characteristics of the majority culture in various aspects of their lives. In social relationships, for example, they may act and think like members of the middle class with whom they now associate on their jobs. But in other ways—religious practices or relations with the opposite sex—they may continue to adhere to the customs of the class from which they sprang.

It is helpful to think of a culture continuum, with the social behavior and attitudes of the majority culture at one extreme and those of the disadvantaged at the other. The majority culture and the culture of the disadvantaged will be described as they are at the extremes, although individuals, families, and sometimes whole neighborhoods can fall anywhere on this continuum.

The contrasts between the two cultures are most readily seen in large cities with slum areas, in sections of the country where there has been an influx of minority groups, and in those states where the socioeconomic level is well below that of the country as a whole and there is a considerable gap between the "haves" and the "have nots." In the smaller cities and towns of the upper Middle West, and in other areas where educational levels have traditionally been well above average, even the so-called working class will have characteristics near the majority-culture end of the continuum. For this reason this analysis is most meaningful when applied to parts of the country where there are distinct pockets of poverty.

Two studies seem to agree about the characteristics of the disadvantaged as a class even when quite disparate backgrounds are represented. Herbert Gans (1964) gives a thorough analysis of the culture of the disadvantaged in the West End of Boston. Jack Weller (1965) reports on the inhabitants of the Southern Appalachian Mountain region, a large percentage of whom have lived all their lives at a subsistence level. The description of the disadvantaged in the following analysis will be based on these studies.[1]

SOCIAL BEHAVIOR AND ATTITUDES COMPARED

The three aspects of life considered here are the family, peer or reference groups, and the community. In each of these categories the social behavior and attitudes of the majority culture are compared to those of the culture of the disadvantaged.

The Family

Majority. The family in the majority culture is predominantly a nuclear one, made up only of the father and mother and their children. Contacts with grandparents, aunts, uncles, and cousins are usually limited to special occasions and play a secondary role in the social life of family members. There are much more frequent contacts with friends, who are selected because of the interests and concerns that they share with different members of the family.

---

[1]See H. Gans, *The Urban Villagers,* New York: Free Press of Glencoe c/o The Macmillan Company, 1964, pp. 45-119, and J. Weller, *Yesterday's People,* pp. 58-101. Copyright 1965 by The University of Kentucky Press. Used by permission of the publishers.

Depending on the breadth and quality of the parents' education, the family is either child centered, (building many of its activities around the wishes of the children) or it is adult directed (with the parents putting high priorities on guiding their children toward what parents consider a desirable way of life.)

Most of the activities of the majority-culture family are heterosexual with relatively little separation of the sexes in social activities, church and civic relationships, or recreation. And many of the responsibilities in the home are shared without regard to sex. Because this pattern applies to the activities of the children, they grow up with little embarrassment in the company of the opposite sex.

The family consciously relates itself in a positive fashion to groups of all kinds outside itself and seeks opportunities to provide the children with firsthand experiences in such groups. The children grow up feeling a part of the total social environment of their communities and with little or no consciousness of an outside world that is alien or antagonistic to them and to their interests. The school, the church, the job, the government, all become so much a part of their world that majority-culture children may assume that these institutions are there primarily to serve their interests and the interests of those who share their norms. By extension they may come to believe that people may rightly be excluded from sharing the benefits of these institutions if they do not abide by the norms of the dominant group.

Disadvantaged. In the culture of the disadvantaged, the family is usually an extended or expanded one. It includes grandparents, aunts or uncles who have no families of their own to care for them, and even on occasion an adopted cousin or more distant relative.

The family is the focus of fairly regular social gatherings limited almost entirely to relatives and, not infrequently, an "adopted" friend or two. A strong attachment develops toward this family group. The members find in it opportunities for self-expression that are not open to them elsewhere, except in their peer groups. They are lost and homesick away from the family, yet they sometimes feel a minimum of that person-to-person affection for family members that is taken for granted in the middle class, and they are often unable to work cooperatively towards family goals.

In most family activities, the members are completely segregated by sex. The women and girls collect in the kitchen and the men and boys in the living room or on the front porch, and woe be to that individual who oversteps this dividing line. As a consequence, members of one sex grow up ill at ease in the presence of the other.

The disadvantaged family is adult centered. The children are expected early in life to adapt to adult patterns of behavior, and their childhood concerns and activities elicit a minimum of interest on the part of the parents. Children are allowed to participate in family gatherings only so long as they do not draw attention to themselves.

Traditionally, children of the disadvantaged culture were looked upon as assets since they could be put to work to help the family finances. Now that this is no longer the case, too frequently little effort is made to keep them in school and few sacrifices are undertaken for their benefit.

The culture of the disadvantaged generally recognizes only the family and peer or reference groups as parts of its world. All other groups, including the school, the church, the job, the government, are looked upon as being part of the outer world—for which a real sense of antagonism exists. This antagonism is, of course, strengthened by the tendency of most of these community groups to set norms and to meet standards determined not by the disadvantaged but by the majority class.

Among the disadvantaged, black families fit this description but have other characteristics that make their situation unique. For example, they are far more matriarchal in structure than white families. The mother is the breadwinner and decision maker and the father, if recognized at all, plays an insignificant role. This relationship tends to alienate the younger family members even more from the larger society of which they should be a part.

Peer or Reference Groups

Majority. Reference groups in the majority culture are usually built around those special interests that are most important at different times in the life of the individual. For this reason they may change with relative frequency and may even be of a seasonal nature. For example, boys and young men may attach themselves to mixed groups during the summer when activities at the beach are popular, but join quite different groups of their own sex during the fall when sports and hunting are in season.

Reference groups in the majority culture are likely to be heterosexual, particularly at later stages in the life cycle. There will, however, be notable exceptions built around special interests of the different sexes.

Majority-culture reference groups are generally object oriented. They are organized, formally or informally, to achieve a common purpose over and beyond the psychological needs of the individual members. The object may be an abstract principle, such as racial or international understanding; a material goal, such as improvement of income; a cultural object, such as music or art appreciation; or a social goal, such as leadership development.

This object orientation of the members of the majority culture, is a product of early family training. Parents move their children from one group to another to achieve goals that they have set for them. They enroll them in nursery schools, encourage their involvement in Boy Scout and Girl Scout activities, urge them to join hobby clubs, athletic teams, social and literary societies. In time the child accepts this pattern of relationships as normal and moves from group to group with relative ease whenever his interests change.

Since such groups are organized to achieve common goals, their mode of operation encourages cooperative attitudes and teaches the individual to subordinate his personal feelings and desires to the common good.

Disadvantaged. Reference groups in the culture of the disadvantaged may remain relatively unchanged during different life cycles and may even be permanent in areas where social and physical mobility is low. They are usually segregated by sex.

The relation of the individual to the reference group is so all-encompassing that he may reveal contrasting personality characteristics when he is outside the group and be extremely uncomfortable when isolated from it. School children from disadvantaged families are often mild and tractable in school, much to the surprise of their teachers, but boisterous and aggressive when back in their peer groups.

These reference groups provide members with opportunities for displaying, expressing, or acting out their individualities—behavior that is acceptable to the group so long as it does not become too extreme. For this reason the members are more interested in activities in which they can impress each other than in achieving common goals that would require them to subordinate their personalities to the group. They actually become competitive in their relationships with each other and find it impossible to cooperate for fear they may be taken advantage of by another member who is seeking personal advantage.

It is the personal relationships within such groups that count. Members need the group in order to become themselves. When circumstances force them to act together as a unit, their concern is only with what common action will do to them as individuals, not with the achievement of goals.

All this dependency makes it difficult for the individuals to develop a self-image apart from the group. They cannot visualize others as thinking or feeling differently, either, and find it hard to see other points of view.

Reference groups among the disadvantaged thrive on action, the "kicks" so often referred to by teenagers. Members are willing to forego day-to-day necessities for these momentary satisfactions. It is in these moments that they are able to express their personalities to the full within the group, and they gain lasting satisfaction from the constant telling and retelling of these moments of glory.

As a consequence of this orientation, routine activities such as going to school and holding down a job become almost unbearable. And this difficulty is compounded by the fact that the kind of achievements that might win them recognition in school and on the job fit middle-class behavior norms that put them at a disadvantage.

Community

Majority. In the dominant culture the community is looked on as an extension of one's reference groups. It provides a wider field for those self-fulfilling activities that are required for the healthy development of the individual. In the organizational activities of the community, the citizen achieves the highest measure of prestige, the fullest exercise of his leadership skills, and the broadest experience of both social and business contacts.

As the citizen's field of action, the community elicits from him a high degree of loyalty. This loyalty, however, is usually directed toward that category of individuals with whom he is most closely involved in his community activities. If his contacts with others have a business orientation, his loyalties go to the business community and he often excludes from consideration other aspects of community life and particularly other individuals who do not share his business affiliations. The same is true of individuals with religious, educational, or social orientations. Only a few persons see the community as a whole and devote their energies to its overall development.

Disadvantaged. Members of the disadvantaged culture have little attachment to the community as such. They see it only as the locale of their special reference-group activities; community institutions are important only insofar as they serve the needs of the peer groups. Church and school activities, for example, have little meaning for them beyond providing opportunities for reference-group contacts.

Even when community activities are intended to meet the special needs of the disadvantaged, the members of this class find it difficult to participate, primarily because they are unaccustomed to subordinating themselves to the direction of leaders. Furthermore, the routine activities required to carry out community goals run contrary to their action orientation. They may show interest at the start, but become easily bored when they realize that persistent effort is required.

Furthermore, members of the culture of the disadvantaged are suspicious of their members who have contacts with what they consider to be the outside world—including those who become involved in community activities. They look upon these individuals as exploiters who may try to manipulate them for personal advantage.

They expect problems to be solved, if at all, by individuals, by their reference groups, or by the favors of politicians. If none of these succeed in finding a solution, members of the disadvantaged culture become resigned and believe the problem is insoluble.

A good deal of this class's antagonism to the community and the outside world is due to its expectation that it will be exploited by them. Historically, there is sufficient evidence to justify such an attitude. It is hard for members of this class to believe that this may no longer be true; they will hardly change their attitude until they see concrete evidence to the contrary. Unfortunately, those who benefit directly from the good will of the outside world tend to move out of the culture of the disadvantaged. Not only does this mean that no one stays around to prove that the outside world can be helpful, but the loss of former associates in this way increases the resentment of the rest.

BRIDGING THE CULTURE GAP

This analysis of the cultures of the majority and of the disadvantaged is very much simplified, of course. Many exceptions to it can be found, as well as wide variations due to ethnic, geographical, and other factors. As mentioned before, blacks are a special case, due not to innate differences so much as to the social conditions under which they have been forced to live. Because of their skin color, their physical and social mobility has been restricted and their job opportunities limited, and they have also been subjected to personal indignities that snuff out the spark of hope. These conditions are being changed, but not fast enough to be of much help to some members of the race. Despite these differences, however, the previous analysis can be applied to blacks as well as to whites all along the continuum.[1]

Awakening people's interest is fundamental to involving them in change efforts. Much can be accomplished in this direction through group activity in various aspects of people's lives—sports, education, employment, business, entertainment, religion, etc. Parents in the

---

[1]For a fuller discussion of this problem, see Appendix I.

majority culture (at least those at the farthest extreme) go to considerable effort to see that their children are involved at a very early age in group activities that can be said to be object oriented, that is, that have as their goals the development of the children's bodies, moral attitudes, skills, and interests. As the children progress through elementary and high school, they are encouraged to continue this process so that by the time they reach adulthood they have developed a variety of interests that they can best satisfy by being involved in the activities of different groups.

On the other hand, the children of the disadvantaged often grow up in areas where such interest groups are much less in evidence. Other than occasionally involving the children as helpers in work activities, their parents seldom concern themselves about the all-round development of the young. The school systems that the children attend, operating as they do on limited budgets, provide few consciously organized efforts to develop skills or interests. When not in class the children are left to their own devices, often without even the equipment needed for group recreation or entertainment. They have little chance to learn what it means to cooperate toward team goals. The informal gangs to which they belong generally subordinate the interest factor to the satisfaction of emotional needs. As a consequence, on reaching adulthood, the disadvantaged have little regard for formal object-oriented group activities of any kind. They become the "uninterested"—the fringe members of community life.

What also must be recognized, however, is that many young people even from the middle class fail to develop any high degree of interest in object-oriented group activities. While our better schools are making efforts (although sometimes in misguided ways) to involve all students in extracurricular activities, where such an interest can be developed, many, many schools throughout the country provide such activities only for the exceptional students, who often make up less than 20 percent of the student body. There are athletic teams and musical, dramatic, literary, and journalistic organizations; in rural areas there are FFA and 4-H programs, but these as a rule do not involve the run-of-the-mill students or those who may be interested but lack the transportation to get home when the school buses are no longer running. These latter students often grow up without developing a strong interest in organized group activities. If they go to college, they continue to remain outsiders, although some may participate in professional organizations related to their chosen fields of study. It is not surprising, therefore, that a relatively low percentage of the total population of any community makes up the membership of its formal organizations, including the churches, and that the same people are found in many different organizations. The rest are the "uninterested" and rarely can be involved in object-oriented change activities.

Rather than concluding that some people are interested in group activities and some are not, the interest factor can be located on the culture continuum. Those who represent the polar extreme of the majority culture will generally show a high degree of interest in various object-oriented group activities, and this interest will decrease along the continuum toward the end representing the culture of the disadvantaged.

Leaders of community organizations attempting to bring about community-wide development or improvement programs must, therefore, be wary of assuming that the members of their organization are homogeneous and share their own attachment to the group's activities and objectives. To gain broad support, leaders must go beyond such object-oriented goals and place major emphasis on meeting the psychological needs of their members. The interest factor will grow as these psychological needs are met. How this can be done will be dealt with in Chapter 14.

REFERENCES AND READINGS

Ball, R. A. A poverty case: The analgesic culture of the southern Appalachians. In I. A. Spergel (Ed.), *Community organization*. Beverly Hills, Calif.: Sage Publications, 1972.

Brager, G., & Specht, H. Mobilizing the poor for social action. In R. M. Kramer & H. Specht (Eds.), *Readings in community organization practice*. Englewood Cliffs, N.J.: Prentice-Hall, 1969.

Cartwright, D. *Human Relations*. New York: Plenum Publishing, 1951.

Edelston, H. C., & Kolodner, F. K. Are the poor capable of planning for themselves? In H. B. C. Spiegel (Ed.), *Citizen participation in urban development*. Washington, D.C.: Center for Community Affairs, 1968.

Gans, H. *The urban villagers*. New York: Free Press of Glencoe, 1964.

Hunter, F. Power structure of a sub-community. In M. Aiken & P. E. Mott (Eds.), *The structure of community power*. New York: Random House, 1970.

Rose, A. The American black: Contexts of ethnic change. In R. Nisbet (Ed.), *Social change*. Oxford: Basil Blackwell, 1972.

Weller, J. *Yesterday's people*. Lexington, Ky.: University of Kentucky Press, 1965.

4

CHANGE AND THE POWER STRUCTURE

No study of planned change would be complete without some consideration of the role of power in the community. Both the will to change and the will to maintain the status quo will vary greatly from community to community, depending on the attitudes and values of the people in positions of power and influence.

THE NATURE OF POWER STRUCTURES

It was long assumed that communities were dominated by a single power structure forming something like a pyramid, with the ultimate power resting at the top. This implied that one or more people, families, or business interests had veto power over the decisions that affected the life of the community. In a few isolated rural communities and particularly in company towns this may still be true. These single power structures, as a rule, straddle institutional lines. For example, those who dominate the business and industrial affairs of a small city or town may be able, by economic means, to exercise control over the political, religious, and educational aspects of the community as well. These individuals can be called the "influentials." In arriving at their decisions they are rarely able to divorce community interests from their own and those of their class.

But these situations are far less common than they used to be. In most of the larger and more complex communities there are a number of power structures that develop along different institutional lines and that effectively counterbalance one another.

The nature of the power structure in any community will be greatly affected by the degree of mobility of people into and out of the area. The more mobility there is, the greater the likelihood that the power structure or structures will be controlled by individuals with *achieved* status, that is, status based on the contributions each person has made to the organizational life of the community. The less mobility there is, particularly into the community, the more the decision making will be dominated by people with *ascribed* status, that is, status assumed without any immediate effort on the possessor's part. Such status is usually based on family, inherited wealth, political connections, or those achievements, not relevant to community needs, that are rated highly in the American value system: fame as a writer, actor, sports hero, or moneymaker. Those with ascribed status may be insulated by their more affluent life style from awareness of community problems and make little or no contribution to their solution; in fact, these individuals may be a major cause of difficulties.

In a small community a few families with ascribed status may constitute the power structure and have such a strangle hold on economic life as to reduce mobility into the community to a minimum. By refusing to rent or sell needed real estate for development purposes, they can effectively keep out industries or business that would bring in outsiders of advanced skill or education. In this way, the influentials prevent their dominance of public decision making from being challenged by more capable, community-minded leadership. Today, however, throughout the nation, factors are operating over which local influentials have no control. Veterans returning from military service with ideas gleaned from the larger world, to take one familiar example, may bring into a previously isolated community a will to change and the know-how to carry it through that will erode the monopoly of power by a few and force them to share the control of local affairs with others. Furthermore, few communities today are impervious to the effects of the mass media. The rising expectations inculcated in all classes by constant exposure to radio, television, and the press have brought concomitant stirrings of determination to break through the artificial barriers that prevent the sharing of the good life by all.

THE ROLE OF THE INFLUENTIALS

Professional planners and community developers often think of planned change almost exclusively in terms of technological changes, which require large sums of money or other concessions from local business organizations or favors of various kinds from political bodies at the county, state, or federal level. The success of such undertakings often depends, therefore, more on the involvement of local influentials than on representatives of the man on the street. Planners who have brought about change under these circumstances are prone to assume that all change can best be achieved only with and through the involvement of the influentials. Or they may become so dependent on the influentials that they are unable to involve a more representative body of citizens when working on changes that demand broad citizen support.

It is important not to ignore the role that influentials can play in certain categories of planned change, but it is equally important to recognize that many changes require a great deal more than money or political clout. For full implementation, change requires a thorough revision of the attitudes, values, and behavior patterns of those citizens who are farthest removed from the power structure; it will be achieved only when these segments of the population are involved in the decision-making process. Many programs related to mental and physical health, family care, and the needs of adolescents and of the aging fall into this category.

THREE TYPES OF COMMUNITY POWER

To avoid antagonizing the influentials, who often can prevent change efforts from getting off the ground, and at the same time to involve those who can get things done, planners need to take a closer look at the community power structure. There are three kinds of power in every community—power here meaning simply the capacity to control the decisions of others.

Power of Legitimate Authority

According to social scientists the first kind of community power is the power of legitimate authority, that is, power given to individuals through elective or appointive offices. Members of county boards of supervisors and town councils hold this kind of power, as do officials in both rural and urban areas. Often such bodies are quite arbitrary in their use of power as long as the electorate remains unorganized on the issues at stake. However, as soon as the councilors or supervisors recognize that opinion is crystallizing within citizen groups that have voting potential, they become more amenable to the wishes of the public.

Those who have legitimate authority are usually jealous of any other groups that seem to be trying to usurp decision-making powers. Attempts by autonomous groups to bring about much-needed change, therefore, will be more likely to succeed when their objectives are first cleared with the local authorities, when their manifest purpose is to study the issue at hand and to make recommendations to the appropriate decision makers, and finally, when change-oriented representatives of legitimate authority are invited early in the planning stages to participate in the study program.

Most supervisory boards are swamped with problems too numerous to receive the attention they deserve. Efforts by local citizen groups to lay some groundwork in specific problem areas usually receive enthusiastic support from official boards. Problems for which there are no easy answers, such as drug abuse and juvenile delinquency, are among many on which help is welcomed. With the additional support of local voluntary organizations, the recommendations of citizen task forces are more likely to be accepted by official boards, as they then have the assurance that they can count on the community at large to implement the recommendations.

Power of Influence

The second type of community power is the power of influence, which rests not on the role the individual is assigned to play by the group, but on his skills, his knowledge, his personality, and the willingness of other people to follow his leadership. The power of influence can be a corollary of achieved status. However, influence can also be a concomitant of ascribed status as, for example, when others are influenced by a person's wealth or family regardless of any genuine contributions the individual makes to the community. Too often, when agencies of government try to identify leaders at the local level, through so-called leadership surveys, they come up with individuals whose influence is due to their ascribed status only. Their influence is often taken for granted by themselves and by others, but it can be totally divorced from the skills needed to get things done.

Power of Coercion

The third type of community power is the power of coercion; it is the ability to force others to act through economic or other forms of pressure, some of which may not be looked upon with favor in our society but have not been challenged effectively at the local level. The ability of certain families, corporations, or labor organizations to maintain a strangle hold on the economic development of their communities rests on this type of power.

There are two significant characteristics of those who depend on the power of coercion. First, they are themselves subject to coercive powers. In recent years minority groups of various kinds, formerly thought of as being completely at the mercy of others, have demonstrated that they, too, can resort to coercive methods to achieve their objectives. Perhaps exposure to the world outside their own communities convinced them that the American Constitution did not sanction their total subjection to the will of others. Second, the tendency of those who exercise coercive power to concentrate on immediate goals of a purely selfish nature often blinds them to the possibilities of even greater benefits which can be achieved through cooperation with others. Encouraging these leaders to study alternatives can sometimes help them to recognize where their best interests coincide with those of the community.

COPING WITH THE POWER STRUCTURE

In small, relatively isolated communities the power of legitimate authority may belong to those individuals who hold the power of coercion or the power of ascribed influence, or both. In this case they may constitute that single power structure mentioned at the beginning of this chapter, which is made up of those properly referred to as the "influentials." As communities become larger and more complex in their social structure, however, the three kinds of power tend to become separated and form parts of several power structures that can counterbalance each other. Certain individuals in any community may combine both the power of legitimate authority and the power of achieved influence, in which case the results are likely to be beneficial to the community as a whole. This means that people in positions of authority who are known and respected for their competence and real leadership skills will have the ready support of the citizens in whatever they undertake.

There is no easy formula for dealing with power structures of either the simple or the complex type. Recognition must be given to the fact, however, that individuals holding any kind of power will have varying degrees of interest in, and concern for, community development or other forms of planned change. People with power of any kind are human beings and have very real differences. To credit all of them with similar limitations or intentions is to misinterpret human nature. Even the term *influential* is a loaded term as applied to many of them. There will be wide variations in their motivation. Some will see that their own interests coincide with those of the community at large and will be willing to exert whatever influence they may have to improve the life of the community. If they are rejected or ignored, however, opportunities for worthwhile change may be lost.

REFERENCES AND READINGS

Bachrach, P., & Baratz, M. S. Two faces of power. In W. D. Hawley & F. M. Wirt (Eds.), *Search for community power*. Englewood Cliffs, N.J.: Prentice-Hall, 1974.

Cahn, E. S., & Cahn, J. C. Citizen participation. In H. B. C. Spiegel (Ed.), *Citizen participation in urban development*. Washington, D.C.: Center for Community Affairs, 1968.

Goldblatt, H. Arguments for and against citizen participation in urban renewal. In H. B. C. Spiegel (Ed.), *Citizen participation in urban development*. Washington, D.C.: Center for Community Affairs, 1968.

Mann, L. D. Studies in community decision making. In R. M. Kramer & H. Specht (Eds.), *Readings in community organization practice*. Englewood Cliffs, N.J.: Prentice Hall, 1969.

Mott, P. E. Power, authority and influence. In M. Aiken and P. E. Mott (Eds.), *The structure of community power*. New York: Random House, 1970.

5

THE PROFESSIONAL CHANGE
AGENT'S APPROACH TO CHANGE

Most of the change efforts in our society are initiated by the paid employees of state and federal agencies and of some voluntary associations. In the field of health alone, the sole purpose of any number of agencies is to organize programs aimed at upgrading the health practices of the people and providing better community health facilities. They are assisted in this by the Red Cross and a variety of local health councils, many of which have paid employees.

These employees of government agencies and voluntary organizations can be referred to as professional change agents. It is their job to facilitate the changes in individual attitudes and practices that are required if their respective institutional objectives are to be attained. Sometimes they go outside their agencies, often to the universities, for technically trained individuals to provide needed skills and information and to stimulate motivation. Insofar as these outsiders are involved in change efforts, they, too, can be called professional change agents.

Since so much social action in America today depends on stimulation and guidance from these professional change agents, it is important that we consider what factors make them effective in their role. These characteristics apply equally well to the professional and the nonprofessional change agent—with one important difference. The latter has much less reason to subordinate human needs to the perpetuation of the agency or organization with which he is identified.

MENTAL ATTITUDES
THAT STIMULATE CHANGE

Expertise in a given field does not, by itself, qualify a person to be a successful change agent; in fact, frequently it proves a handicap.

Likewise, success as an administrator, writer, researcher, or university professor too often fosters an attitude that discourages rather than encourages others to accept the change being advocated.

This was not always so. In an earlier day when the general population was not highly educated, the well-educated man with status in his community was eagerly sought for his help in solving public and private problems.

Today people generally are better educated and, through the mass media, have ready access to a store of knowledge, some accurate and some not. As a result, they question the ultimate wisdom of any one person, particularly if he overlooks the knowledge and experience of those he is trying to help. From their point of view, the expert can easily become a person who knows all the answers but does not quite understand the questions.

Today the change agent needs more than just a mastery of facts. He needs to acquire special attitudes toward his fellows.

The average individual in his role as administrator, professor, researcher, or specialist deals with the public according to the code of conduct that is taken for granted by his professional colleagues and that he may feel is essential to his status role. He may be reluctant at first to reshape his approach to accommodate unfamiliar, and admittedly idealistic, attitudes toward others. But when his efforts to stimulate change run into resistance from those with whom he is working, he will find it to his advantage to adopt these attitudes.

THE NINE BASIC ATTITUDES OF THE CHANGE AGENT

Nine basic attitudes appropriate to the effective change agent are listed here.[1]

1. He accepts the fact that life is so complex that, however expert he is in his chosen field, there are almost always people in the groups he is working with who have had related experiences and who possess relevant information that he does not have, particularly about the local situation. He treasures this information and encourages these people to share it with the other members of the group.

2. As he gains mastery of his chosen field he is not deluded that he knows enough. He constantly tries to broaden his horizons

---

[1] I am indebted to Drs. Harry and Bonaro Overstreet who, in a talk they gave years ago on sound mental health, provided the basic ideas from which these attitudes are derived. Dr. Bonaro Overstreet has given her gracious permission to adapt these ideas to the present purpose.

to encompass understandings that give new meaning to all aspects of life. A technician who is first and foremost a technical expert is not suited to be an effective change agent.

3. He constantly seeks to enlarge the circle of his fellow men for whom he can feel genuine compassion. He recognizes his role of change agent as providing an incomparably unique opportunity for bringing this about. If it is hard for him to feel compassion for people outside his immediate family or social circle, he works doubly hard to put himself in other people's shoes whenever he deals with them.

4. As his ultimate objective is to bring about change, and not to gain a popular following, he puts communicating with others above entertaining or impressing them with his erudition and cleverness. He makes sure that he has something worth communicating, that he uses comprehensible language free of jargon, professionalese, and meaningless generalities. He resists the temptation to use communication aids of any kind, no matter how impressive, unless they clarify the meaning of what he is presenting. He limits humor to what will put his audience at ease and facilitate the communication process.

5. He helps the people he works with to accept unpleasant situations that they cannot change. When disasters or disappointments come, he helps others to look at those elements of the situation that present new challenges to them. Often enough they find that what they wanted so much would have been a setback, viewed from the standpoint of their total life experience. And, of course, before he can genuinely deal with the setbacks of others in this way, he has made this point of view a part of his own working philosophy.

6. He accepts his own limitations and helps others to do the same, and he starts by declining to undertake the leadership responsibilities that too often are assumed by change agents as a matter of course. He directs the attention of group members to developing more fully the talents they already have. This becomes increasingly important as he tries to involve more and more people in the democratic process of planned change. Many will want to be what they are not qualified to be, while they ignore their capacities that are unique and needed by the group. Others use personal limitations as an excuse for not becoming involved in civic responsibilities. They need the change agent's encouragement to develop a more constructive frame of mind.

7. He keeps his emotions and his impulses under control and sets the pattern for the conduct of the groups with which he works. Regardless of his leadership role, he resists the temptation to expect preferential acceptance of his ideas and in no case indulges in "throwing his weight around." He is especially careful not to use his knowledge or his position to make some-one feel small.

8. He constantly raises the question of how he and his fellows can work for the common good even when this means giving up some of their own personal gratifications. Together they try to recognize where this society has been at fault in the past to cause it to be in the sorry position it is in today, not only in regard to the fast-deteriorating physical environment but also in regard to unfortunate human relationships. The change agent tries to reverse the trend not by telling others what needs to be done, but by helping them discover for themselves what is in their own and the nation's best interest in the long run. Helping others to subordinate their individual expecta-tions to the common good becomes one of his first and most difficult responsibilities. Only if he can demonstrate that it is a dominant factor in his own philosophy of life can he hope to be effective in bringing about needed changes.

9. Finally, he values other people's time as highly as his own. When he has a key role to play in any program, he is never late on the excuse that the meeting cannot begin without him. By his example he helps group members build a greater respect for the value of each other's time not only by starting but also by stopping on schedule. In ongoing programs, he seeks the consensus of the group as to whether the scheduled hours are convenient. He knows that citizens frequently become lax about being on time when schedules have been arbitrarily set by professional people whose needs are quite different from their own and that they stay away from group sessions when those in charge give every evidence of having no built-in "terminal facilities."

These then are the attitudes that the professional and the non-professional change agent alike will need to cultivate in order to be most effective in the democratic process of planned change. While they constitute ideals that may never be perfectly achieved, the change agent's determination to shape his conduct by them will in good time become evident to those he works with and win for him satisfactions in his personal relations that could never be achieved in any other way.

By his own increasing maturity of mind he is making it possible for others to achieve maturity and fulfillment along with him. This is the essence of planned change in a democratic society.

REFERENCES AND READINGS

Cary, L. J. Role of the professional community developer. *Journal of the Community Development Society*, 1972, Vol. 3, No. 2, 36-41.

Ross, M. G. *Community organization*. New York: Harper & Row, 1955.

Sanders, I. T. Professional roles in planned change. In R. Kramer & H. Specht (Eds.), *Readings in community organization practice*. Englewood Cliffs, N.J.: Prentice-Hall, 1969.

Schaller, L. E. *The change agent*. New York: Abingdon Press, 1972.

6

DEALING WITH CONTROVERSY IN THE CHANGE PROCESS

CONTROVERSY AND THE CHANGE AGENT

Attempts at planned change are often resisted by both agencies and private groups because at some time in the past such change efforts have led to open controversy and, to use a familiar phrase, have "split the community wide open." Even when an agency takes a neutral position, the fact that it has been instrumental in raising the issue can cause serious repercussions, particularly if the agency depends on local political bodies for part or all of its financial support. As a result, many agencies, as a matter of policy, shy away from any potentially controversial issue.

However, almost any topic that provokes opposing views can be considered controversial, and to oppose change for this reason can completely nullify an agency's responsibilities as a change agent.

Professional change agents will discover that however practical, rational or scientific a topic may be from their point of view, it is apt to be looked at in a different light by many of those they are trying to influence. Perhaps daily exposure to mass media, particularly television, has given many people just enough information, or misinformation, to justify their having opinions on almost every topic under the sun, and they see no reason for taking a back seat to anyone else in a discussion. The day has long since passed when the many were expected to defer to the wisdom of a few.

PRESENTATION OF ISSUES AND CONTROVERSY

Whether topics of discussion lead to controversy depends, however, not so much on the topics themselves, but on the conditions under which they are presented.

There are four main reasons why almost any topic of consequence can lead to controversy.

1. *The issue as presented to the public:*
   - is not recognized as a felt need by local people;
   - is not supported by enough factual information to which the public has ready access.

2. *The issue as presented to the public:*
   - does not represent a problem but one of a number of solutions to a problem not yet clearly identified;
   - introduces a new element in the existence of the group, such as government controls (e.g., zoning ordinances) where no such controls have existed before;
   - involves a change that can too readily be dubbed as communistic, socialistic, middle class, or un-American.

3. *The issue as seen by the public:*
   - contains a great deal of misinformation, which may be nothing more than generally accepted attitudes such as, for example, the superiority of the white race or the dominant role of the male in our society;
   - consciously misinterprets facts to strengthen the hands of those who wish to maintain the status quo;
   - is merely a good vote getter for politicians interested in developing a local following;
   - is opposed for selfish reasons by moneyed groups that may have a narrow concept of their own best interests.

4. *The individuals recognized as advocating change include:*
   - persons readily identified as outsiders who may, therefore, be assumed to have questionable motives;
   - those who can be typed by their dress, hair style, jargon, or mannerisms as not being "one of us" by local people—these may include some so-called experts brought in to help engineer the change;
   - specialists inclined to take a "know-it-all" attitude toward the issue and put a low value on local knowledge and experience;
   - bureaucrats supporting untested "ideal" solutions, some details of which would be detrimental to certain classes of people (a model rural zoning ordinance, for example, proposed by a state community affairs agency, which was never submitted to farmers for review and which includes a clause forbidding the construction of structures taller than the primary buildings on county properties, thus making it un-

lawful for a farmer to build a barn or silo higher than the ranch-style house in which he lives);
- individuals who, because of their professional status in the community, presume to be experts on every topic imaginable and do not listen to others.

These causes of controversy could have been avoided in most cases had the change agent or agents responsible for initiating change done the following:

- Involved a representative group of local citizens from a wide range of organizations and from various institutional backgrounds in identifying and defining the basic problems;
- Concentrated their efforts not on gaining acceptance of their pet solutions but on seeing that the group process permitted members to arrive at their conclusions in a democratic and logical manner;
- Responded to requests for information, whenever possible, by providing alternative choices and their expected consequences so that citizens could choose the situation best suited to their needs and capabilities;
- Brought in only outside experts who could present information in a straight-forward, objective manner compatible with local customs and feelings.

FURTHER UNDERLYING CAUSES OF CONTROVERSY

Controversy Along Socioeconomic Lines

When members of a community are divided largely along socioeconomic lines on a given issue, much of the opposition from the low-income members can arise because they have had no previous opportunity to get involved in the community's decision-making process. With little experience in formal group activities, attempts to bring them into community meetings have often proved disastrous, as much for their interests as for those of the community at large. If the issue is an important one, it would pay to conduct some neighborhood sessions among low income groups to get them to identify their needs in relation to the issue at hand and to define the problem from their point of view. The use of trained facilitators, preferably selected from among them, will help in conducting these small-group discussions. If the individuals who are chosen to represent the low-income groups are recognized as the most capable of expressing themselves effectively, the chances will be greater that the resulting decisions will be acceptable to all. Low-income groups should not be encouraged to formulate ahead of time their own solutions to the problems under consideration. If they do, their decisions can too readily become "demands" in their eyes and the eyes of the rest of the community, and make compromise more difficult. There is good reason, on the other hand, for a clear statement of the problem as seen from their point of view.

Resisting Change

Almost everyone resists change when it touches his life directly at the community or neighborhood level. Habitual life patterns give a sense of security essential to a person's well-being. He prefers the familiar to the unknown.

A great many people regard the norms of their particular culture or subculture as the only acceptable ones and find it hard to believe that people can live satisfactory lives under other conditions. Proposed changes that are "obviously" to their advantage from an outsider's point of view may not seem so to them and will be resisted. Perceptions are distorted by cultural heritage.

In every community in America there are merchants, real estate developers, politicians, and others who are not so much opposed to change as to those particular changes that might interfere with their own already-established objectives, which can often be summed up in one word—profits. Proposals by community leaders to achieve sound community development become barriers to "progress" and to the proper functioning of the free enterprise system as these special groups interpret it.

Some citizens fail to see how proposed changes can be related to their own needs or, if sacrifices are called for, how any sacrifices can benefit them. Elderly people living on fixed incomes, for example, frequently oppose having to pay increased taxes for improved school systems because they do not recognize the relationship between better education and lower crime rates and welfare costs.

When community goals are stated abstractly, as they so frequently are with terms like "improvement" or "development," many people fail to find them sufficiently meaningful to merit support. And if attempts at change in the past were poorly organized and resulted in failure, some people who were enthusiastic supporters may prove hostile to further efforts. They do not want to repeat what was for them a frustrating and embarrassing experience.

All of us have culturally acquired attitudes about those who differ from us in race, religion, sex, national origin, or socioeconomic class. Often these attitudes make it difficult for us to treat those who are not of our kind as if they were human beings like ourselves. Some of our prejudices are based on myths that have gone unchallenged for generations; others are based on the limited contacts that we have had with members of the subcultures in our society. Becoming involved in non-controversial activities with people who are different from ourselves does not always break down these prejudices, but it can help pave the way to cooperation in solving common problems when they arise. Too frequently our first confrontations with people from other subcultures occur when we have already taken sides on a given issue. Then it is too late.

COPING WITH CONTROVERSY
Dealing with Those Who Are Resistant to Change

In any community situation where changes are proposed by the more "progressive" elements in the population, there will be others who resist change for one or more of the preceding reasons. A sense of being under attack by the forces of change can cause such groups to seek security together despite wide differences in socioeconomic and educational levels. The individuals who make up these mutual-security organizations become almost impervious to reasonable discussion and, in fact, are determined to keep it from taking place. Separately they might be dealt with effectively; united this is no longer possible.

In situations where a few determined individuals seek to bring about planned change—however legitimate or worthy—the usual approach is for them to "gang up" and prevent opposition spokesmen from airing their views. As a consequence, members of the opposition will unite with anyone who agrees with them on the issue even if they disagree in other respects. This unity strengthens their will to resist on the one hand while minimizing their individual reasons for opposing change. At this point someone usually "whips up" the opposition forces with slogans and an overall objective and the efforts for change are often defeated.

Such an impasse can be avoided if, when change is contemplated and the community is still in the process of identifying the problem that confronts it, representatives of all segments of the population participate and express their reactions at every step—not in large groups where a few can dominate, but in small discussion groups where all can speak openly and freely. In this way, negative reactions to the change can be aired and dealt with rationally. Misconceptions and misinformation can be cleared up. Not all opposition can be overcome in this way, but those who hold uncompromising positions can be isolated. Their general intransigence can be exposed for what it is, and they will have less appeal to those who might have joined forces with them.

People who habitually play the role of blocker usually do so to satisfy their need for recognition. In a group of only half a dozen people, however, this need is never fully satisfied and they find their blocking tactics wasted.

(It needs to be noted that some thoughtful people have valid reasons for opposing change. But when these reasons are presented in the often emotion-charged atmosphere of the usual public hearing, they are frequently ignored or their importance is minimized by the advocates of change. On such occasions, valuable information may be lost and the groundwork laid for problems that will rise later to plague the community.)

Also in small groups the influence of traditional leaders who are satisfied with the status quo is considerably diminished. Their unsupported statements or meaningless generalities will be seen for what they are and, when voting takes place, it will be based on the merits of the case rather than on the position of the person who originated it.

Avoiding the Roadblocks of Controversy

The most common mistake of professional people dealing with community concerns is to assume that "the facts speak for themselves." They measure their success by the number of people who have been exposed to the facts (as the expert sees them, of course), not by the amount of change that has taken place. The result of this is dispute over "the facts" and diminished chances of achieving fruitful change. With planning, however, such roadblocks can be avoided.

The Exploratory Committee Approach

A change agent could well start by calling together an exploratory committee of six to a dozen carefully chosen, change-oriented, local leaders to get their frank reaction to the topic and to the "facts" as he sees them. If he shows himself willing to incorporate their suggestions, and to modify his approach to fit local conditions, he should be able to count on their future support. They will accept the idea, at least in part, as their own.

He can then enlist their help in setting up a community-wide, problem-identification workshop. If he has not tried to manipulate his exploratory group, the problem will surface in the workshop and it will then be recognized as a felt need by the community. After that it will be up to the community to decide whether it has top priority and deserves further consideration.

Relating Issues to Audience Readiness

Occasionally agencies or voluntary organizations want to arouse interest in an important problem that citizens have not given much thought to. They may even be unaware of its significance to the community.

People may react negatively if they are expected to handle a problem they are not ready to deal with. If they have just heard about an issue for the first time, yet are asked to make a decision about it, they may resist or reject it for fear that their ignorance of the subject will be exposed. This resistance may often take irrational forms and lead to open controversy.

Considerable research over the years has revealed that there are several stages in people's reactions to new ideas (Fessler, 1966).[1]

1. *Information getting*
   a. the awareness stage—they have just heard about it.
   b. the interest stage—they want to know more.
2. *Learning*
   a. the evaluation stage—they want to try it out mentally.
   b. the trial stage—they want to put it into practice on a small scale.
3. *Decision making*
   a. the adopting stage—they accept the idea until a better one comes along.

Group Involvement

In moving from the awareness stage to the adoption stage, an individual's decision-making powers are increasingly called into play and it is important that he become more and more involved in the decision making of the group. The five stages of people's reactions to new ideas can be placed on a continuum, with low-audience involvement at one end and high-audience involvement at the other. Such a continuum is illustrated in Figure 6.1.

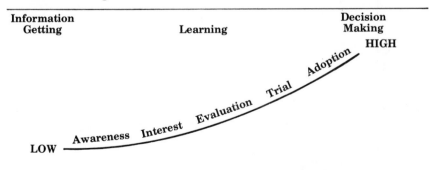

Fig. 6.1. Audience Involvement at Different
Stages of Reactions to New Ideas

[1]Donald R. Fessler, "Meetings," in THE COOPERATIVE EXTENSION SERVICE, H.C. Sanders, editor, © 1966, pp. 145-151. Adapted by permission of Prentice-Hall, Inc., Englewood Cliffs, New Jersey.

When an idea or issue is first brought to the attention of the public, and presumably there is no need for personal or group decisions about it, the topic can be presented with a minimum of audience involvement. However, when it becomes essential to evaluate the idea, try it out, or finally to adopt it there needs to be increasing involvement of all concerned.

When entire communities are confronted with important issues, the large number of people making up any audience may make involvement difficult. Involvement must then be achieved by the manner in which the program is conducted. Different types of program formats can be placed on a high-low audience-involvement continuum (Figure 6.2).

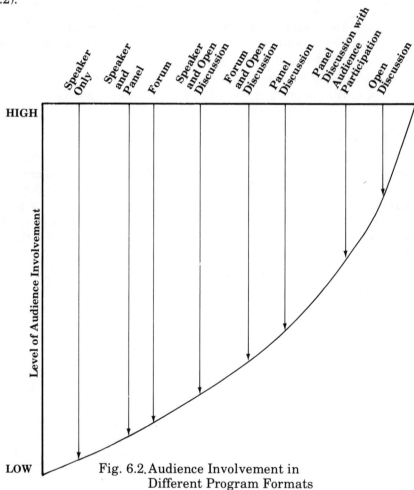

Fig. 6.2. Audience Involvement in
Different Program Formats

A panel is a group that carries on a free discussion without prepared speeches; its success depends on how well it represents the different points of view of the audience. In a forum, each member is given an opportunity to make a formal presentation in a limited length of time.

Even at the awareness stage, when audience involvement need not be high, allowing everyone to discuss the topic and raise questions about it will have the effect of making the topic more meaningful, relating it more directly to an individual's own life experience, and arousing his genuine interest in it.

Avoiding Ambiguity

If the audience is small enough, "buzz group" discussions will help eliminate misinterpretations that later can lead to controversy. Time should be allowed at the end of the buzz sessions for each group to ask questions. Some speakers resist submitting to this kind of audience reaction as they are accustomed to saying the last word on a topic. They may be amazed how the audience has interpreted or misinterpreted their remarks and learn from the experience how to avoid such ambiguity. On the other hand, they could be encouraged by concrete evidence that the audience comprehended what they said and related it to its own experience.

AVOIDING CONTROVERSY: A MATTER OF PROCESS AND TIMING

Beyond the measures already mentioned, there are no pat formulas for dealing with controversy at the community level any more than there are easy ways of dealing with other forms of difficult human behavior. But one encouraging fact should not be overlooked. It is the conditions under which a topic is presented to the public and the manner of its presentation—rather than the topic itself—that arouses resistance and resentment and that can be anticipated and prepared for in advance. However, it is important that community leaders not wait too long before they try to come to grips with an issue on a community-wide basis. The longer they allow a topic to simmer, the more likely it will be that unfavorable conditions will arise that may be beyond their power to control. People will take sides, the unprincipled with vested interests will disseminate untruths or half truths, and the less thoughtful members of the community will allow others to appeal to their loyalty and their emotions and stifle what good judgment they may possess. Change agents must be aware of this dilemma and know how to deal with it.

REFERENCES AND READINGS

Carmack, W. R. Communication and community readiness for change. In G. Zaltman, P. Kotler, & I. Kaufman (Eds.), *Creating social change*. New York: Holt, Rinehart & Winston, 1972.

Fessler, D.R. Meetings. In H.C. Sanders (Ed.), *The Cooperative Extension Service.* ©1966, pp. 145-151.

Jenkins, D. H. Force field analysis applied to school situation. In W. G. Bennis, K. D. Benne, & R. Chin (Eds.), *The planning of change*. New York: Holt, Rinehart & Winston, 1962.

Specht, H. Disruptive tactics. In R. M. Kramer & H. Specht (Eds.), *Readings in community organization practice.* Englewood Cliffs, N.J.: Prentice-Hall, 1969.

Watson, G. Meeting resistance. In G. Zaltman, P. Kotler, & I. Kaufman (Eds.), *Creating social change*. New York: Holt, Rinehart & Winston, 1962.

Zaltman, G., Duncan, R., & Holbek, J. *Innovations and organizations*. New York: John Wiley & Sons, 1973.

Zander, A. T. Resistance to change—its analysis and prevention. In W. G. Bennis, K. D. Benne, & R. Chin (Eds.), *The planning of change*. New York: Holt, Rinehart & Winston, 1962.

7
THE ROLE OF CRISIS AND LEADERSHIP IN CHANGE

There are those who believe that crisis situations must arise before constructive change or effective community development can take place. But there is no proof that crisis, in itself, is essential to planned change. Often community action waits for a crisis situation to develop because the traditional leaders are the last to be touched by deteriorating conditions in their city. They live and work in areas where crime and poverty are not apparent and official corruption does not touch them directly. They awake only when violence or disaster breaks through the barriers.

THE JACKSONVILLE STORY

This is beautifully illustrated by the story of how Jacksonville, Florida, was finally goaded into consolidating the sprawling political units of the second largest metropolitan area in the United States into one overall governmental structure.

Jacksonville's public services had long been deteriorating. Crime was rampant, and corruption of office holders was endemic. Citizens had taken these conditions for granted for years, but when all the city's fifteen high schools lost their accreditation, and sons and daughters of the more prosperous families were no longer automatically admitted to respected colleges and universities, action was in order. This was in 1964.

The revolt was led by a few determined business leaders and one politician who had maintained a reputation for being "Mr. Clean" in politics. With the help of a select group of their fellows, these leaders drafted a manifesto asking the local delegation to the Florida legislature for an act to enable the citizens of the county to vote on a new scheme of government that would bring all governmental units in the county into one. This was their "Declaration of Independence."

At this point real citizen involvement began. Instead of hiring a group of experts to draft an ivory-tower blueprint which would probably be voted down, the "rebels" initiated scores of hearings and formed task forces and subcommittees representing existing volunteer organizations. In this way they hoped to persuade the public that conditions could be different if they chose to make them so; they hoped to produce an entirely new civic structure that the voters would understand and approve. The new structure called for a single, strong, simply organized government for the whole county with a mayor and city council elected by, and therefore responsive to, the people, but with administrative officers appointed by the mayor so that he would have genuine control over the municipal machinery. It also provided for spreading the tax burden fairly over the entire metropolitan area, suburbs and center city alike.

The infighting and maneuvering to overcome the opposition of entrenched politicians and office holders called for some hard choices on the part of many groups in the city. Blacks, for example, had to choose between weakening their voting power in the central city and their desire for decent schools, housing, jobs, and better public services. In the process, values emerged. In the same way, middle-class suburbanites had to choose between maintaining comfortable, adequately serviced, isolated communities and sharing responsibility for the area-wide problems spawned by a bankrupt central city.

After a bitter three-year battle, in 1967 the consolidation proposal was approved in a county-wide referendum by a majority of almost two to one. As John Fischer reported, "The victory was unique. No other American community had succeeded in this century in remodeling its government so completely and at first try."[1]

The economies achieved by merging duplicate city and county agencies and by modernizing the tax structure made it possible for the city not only to reduce taxes but to end its last fiscal year with a four million dollar surplus.

The city's air and waterways were cleaned up; schools were upgraded and regained their accreditation; fire protection improved so markedly that insurance rates came down; ten new health centers were built and mobile clinics were provided for outlying areas; 16,500 streetlights were installed; streets were repaved, particularly in the poorer sections of the towns; new parks, swimming pools, and recreation centers were added; police forces were consolidated and their

---

[1]This description of the Jacksonville story was condensed from an article by John Fischer entitled "Jacksonville, So Different You Can Hardly Believe It," which appeared in *Harper's*, July 1971, p. 24, and was reprinted in *Vital Signs, U.S.A.* New York: Harper & Row, 1975. Used by permission of the publishers.

personnel upgraded; more coherent plans were made for the whole metropolitan area, and the city again became attractive to new industrial and service enterprises.

Without question all of this represented a tremendous change of values on the part of the citizens of Jacksonville. Many skeptics acquired a new perspective as they saw changes for the better take place.

The crisis situation could have led to quite different results. Had the so-called "rebels" followed the course taken by many cities in similar circumstances and called in experts to develop a blueprint for a consolidated metropolitan government, the referendum might very well have been two to one against. Instead, the leaders, who apparently were acquainted with the principles of group process or had knowledgeable consultants, provided situations in which citizens from all over the metropolitan area could communicate their concerns to each other about what they wanted in the way of a government.

A major factor for success in Jacksonville, therefore, was not the crisis but the wisdom of the leaders in involving their fellow citizens, across organizational lines and among political units. Jacksonville's leaders were astute enough to realize that most of the major changes they sought would eventually require approval at the polls. This meant that the least affluent citizen would, in theory at least, carry as much weight as a monied member of the Establishment and needed to be involved in the process from the very start.

THE ROLE OF LEADERSHIP
IN PLANNED CHANGE

A number of examples can be cited where successful planned change has taken place without crisis. Throughout the southeastern part of the United States over the past twenty years most of the states have been conducting community improvement programs in rural areas. These have usually been under the joint sponsorship of state cooperative extension services and local chambers of commerce. Their objectives have been the improvement of homes, farms and other sources of income, and services and organizations within communities. As a rule they have operated on a contest basis.

The hundreds of communities involved are in rural neighborhoods, many of which had not seen any visible, consciously planned changes for generations. When the sponsoring organizations tried to encourage the development of a community improvement club, they were often told that they were wasting their time, that the community had no leaders and, therefore, there was little hope of getting the people to participate in such a program. The sponsors ignored these warnings and sought out individuals who could help identify local needs. Once this was done it was not difficult to find others who would carry out activities necessary to meet these needs. Usually in less than a year most of these communities had thriving improvement organizations operating under the effective guidance of individuals who had never previously thought they had leadership capabilities. At the end of each year the communities were judged on the number and quality of their improvements and the outstanding ones were given regional and statewide recognition and cash awards.

Both in Jacksonville and in these rural neighborhood communities, the key factor in the change efforts lay in organizational procedures that allowed for the broadest possible participation of citizens in decision making and, concomitantly, the wide diffusion of leadership skills.

OUTMODED CONCEPTS OF LEADERSHIP

If the initiators of change, professional or otherwise, operate with outmoded concepts of leadership that have prevailed for generations in most communities, concepts that still dominate the thinking of many people in business and government, then effective change will not take place no matter how serious a crisis a community faces. At the start of any change effort, therefore, those who are asked to lead at any level should be trained in the new concepts of leadership and in the skills of organization necessary to support these concepts.

It will first be useful to take a look at some of the misconceptions of leadership that still prevail in many communities.

Authoritarian Concept

The most prevalent misconception is that authoritarian leader behavior, which is fairly effective and perhaps inevitable in chain-of-command organizations such as business corporations, the military services, and government, can be used in volunteer citizen organizations as well. The leader is responsible for making group decisions and expects the group's support.

Occasionally an authoritarian leader has enough personal magnetism or charisma to carry off the successful operation of a voluntary organization. Such cases are the exception, however, and even when they occur, the group becomes so wholly dependent on the leader that it falls apart as soon as his term of office comes to an end. It has failed to mature and to develop new leaders to take his place. Many churches have been dominated in this way and either have broken up or have become inactive when their ministers left for assignments elsewhere.

And how many chambers of commerce, service clubs, and other volunteer groups have had brief periods of glory under so-called dynamic leaders only to decline when these individuals retired?

In almost all such cases, the psychological needs of the leader are being met while those of the members are ignored because the leaders are individual-centered rather than group-centered. People in the majority culture often tolerate authoritarian leadership of this kind because they believe it is necessary to get the job done and they are more interested in group goals than in members of the group. The ordinary members of most citizen organizations, however, are much less apt to be interested in abstract goals than in the satisfaction of their own psychological needs, even though they may not be consciously aware of this. If these satisfactions are denied by leaders who do not involve members in identifying problems and in making important decisions, members no longer feel impelled to give the group their wholehearted support or even to continue their participation.

Cultural Determinism Theory

A second erroneous concept about leadership is that social situations, such as crises, produce the leaders they require. This is called the *cultural determinism theory* of leadership. The success of such men as Franklin D. Roosevelt, Winston Churchill, and Mahatma Gandhi is seen as support for this theory.

When crisis situations arise, people will often accept the leadership of individuals who offer unique or radical solutions, leaders who were ignored when conditions were normal. But in many crises individuals with the needed skills do not appear. In many developing countries today, conditions have gone from bad to worse because there are no potential leaders with the special skills needed to solve the problems these countries face. There are no leaders because there has been no training in leadership skills. Some newly independent countries in Asia and Africa, for example, lack skilled leaders in government, industry, commerce, education, and many other fields because their former rulers did not encourage the education and training of the native leaders on whom the responsibilities have now fallen.

As crisis situations arise in the ghetto areas of our large cities, potential leaders, trained in democratic procedures, must be available from the culture of the disadvantaged to help solve the problems of the people they represent. If they are not available, demagogues will step in and take control.

The concept that some people are *born* to be leaders and others are not is now generally discredited except among a few in the dominant culture who cling to it as an excuse for not developing indigenous leaders from among the less fortunate classes.

Trait Concept

In recent years the trait concept of leadership has been popular in certain quarters. According to this concept leaders possess various intellectual, physical, and personality traits to a higher degree than do their followers. Considerable research has been carried out to find support for this theory; in twenty different studies, some seventy-nine different "leadership" traits were identified. However, when the results of the studies were compared it was found that only five percent of the traits were common to four or more of the studies. This seems to indicate that what a leader needs most is the particular skill or skills required by his group at a particular point in its development. If he can fill this need, very little else matters.

Situational and Functional Concepts

In contrast to these older concepts of leadership, two relatively new concepts deserve our attention. In the *situational concept*, a leader is a person who is recognized by the group as having the skills it needs and who is put into a situation where he can use these skills to help achieve group goals. In the *functional concept*, leadership is the performance of certain functions required at particular points in a group's operations. Since a group is dynamic and growing and has different needs at different stages of its development, a wide variety of such functions can be exercised in the course of even a short-lived group session. In immature groups many of these functions will be concentrated in the hands of a few individuals, but as the group matures it will operate more efficiently and cooperatively as more and more of the members share in performing them. (See Chapter 16 for a more detailed discussion of these two concepts.)

LAYING THE GROUNDWORK FOR CHANGE

The first consideration of those responsible for initiating change efforts at the community level is to locate a number of group-centered leaders who can put into effect procedures that will strengthen the interpersonal relations of all group members and maximize support for whatever objectives the group selects. Such an individual should be able to:

1. Create a climate that encourages each group member to use his capabilities to the full for the achievement of group goals;
2. Identify inherent resources in the group so that they may be fully utilized;

3. Recognize the individual needs that must be satisfied within the group's activities if the group is to maintain itself;
4. Demonstrate faith that the members of the group know better than he does what their needs are and what capabilities and resources they possess to meet those needs;
5. Encourage the growth of the group as a whole and of each member so that, should he himself have to withdraw from the group, temporarily or otherwise, it could continue its activities without interruption because others are prepared to assume his responsibilities;
6. Make the group's activities so rewarding as a personal experience that there will be a strong desire on the part of all members not to miss any of them.

Obviously this is a big order and one that will not easily be satisfied in most communities. It can, however, be achieved through training. If enough leaders from local voluntary organizations and churches are given the opportunity to undergo relatively short training in effective group techniques, a number will emerge who can fill the responsibilities outlined above and stress a group-centered approach to problem solving and group decision making.

REFERENCES AND READINGS

Bennis, W. G. Leadership theory and administrative behavior. In W. G. Bennis, K. D. Benne, & R. Chin (Eds.), *The planning of change*. New York: Holt, Rinehart & Winston, 1962.

Fischer, J. *Vital signs: U.S.A.* New York: Harper & Row, 1975.

Morris, R. The role of the agent in the community development process. In L. J. Cary (Ed.), *Community development as a process*. Columbia, Mo.: University of Missouri Press, 1970.

Nisbet, R. *Social change*. Oxford: Basil Blackwell, 1972.

Ross, M. G., & Hendry, C. E. *New understandings of leadership*. New York: Association Press, 1957.

8
MAXIMIZING INDIVIDUAL CAPABILITIES
IN CHANGE EFFORTS

Most planned change is task oriented rather than people oriented. It is geared to achieving specific goals such as the creation of a neighborhood recreation center, the consolidation of county political units, or the establishment of a regional water authority. Little thought is given to using the opportunity to develop the decision-making group into a more mature entity and, in the process, enhancing the leadership capabilities of its members. One frequent consequence of this task orientation is that the community is capable of planned change only so long as certain key individuals are present and willing to assume leadership roles. This, in turn, limits the nature and quality of the community's change efforts.

Whenever citizens are brought together to deal with community problems, agreeing on a solution should be only one of the group's objectives. Three others are equally important: (1) to gain the broadest possible community-wide support for whatever decisions are made; (2) to operate so as to maximize the capabilities and fully utilize the resources of members; and (3) to help members overcome whatever handicaps they may have in working with each other. Achieving the second and third objectives will greatly enhance the likelihood of achieving the first.

Social groups are collections of persons who seek to satisfy their individual needs within and through their relationships with each other. Man's special nature derives from his relationship to, and dependence on, groups. His personality grows when he can use his energies to further group goals, in other words, to exercise his leadership capabilities. The more restricted the individual's experience with groups, the more limited his personality growth will be. However, it does not follow that more growth will result from involvement with more groups. It is the character of the relationship that counts. A dominating leader in many community groups may show no more personality growth than the individual who assumes a completely passive role in few groups. Personality growth is directly related to the degree to which an individual learns to help others achieve fulfillment with him in the group activities they share.

Many rural communities, and some disadvantaged neighborhoods in urban centers, offer few formal group relationships outside the family. Those that do exist, such as the church, often have such a limited variety of activities that few members find opportunities to use the capabilities they possess or to develop leadership skills. Such communities are recognized as relatively "dead" by local people as well as outsiders. However, startling changes in the personality growth of community members may take place when these communities organize development or improvement programs (usually under the stimulus of outside forces) that require a wide variety of group activities and unique leadership skills. Some who had previously played passive roles in local activities become effective leaders in areas where they have special skills. Their personalities expand as they take on leadership functions.

However, initiating a community development program will not, by itself, develop the right kind of leadership or stimulate individual growth. Some local individuals who have misconceptions about leadership (see Chapter 8) may undertake to get an improvement program under way. Their approach, if it does not jettison the program at the start, usually minimizes the benefits of group activities on the personality growth of members. In most cases these individuals are conscientiously doing what they think is expected of them as leaders and are not motivated by selfish reasons. If tactfully approached, they may be willing to undergo training in how to work more effectively with groups before they assume leadership responsibilities.

THE FUNDAMENTALS OF GROUP MAKE-UP

There are elements in every group that have a bearing on the personality growth of its members as well as how the group accomplishes its task. Groups differ in the attitudes, values, and forms of behavior they consider acceptable. And within them, interpersonal relations will be greatly affected by two factors that operate differently from group to group: member status and the power of members to control the group.

The way a group looks upon an individual's status limits his effectiveness. Some groups make it possible to acquire status by the amount an individual contributes to its activities. Substantial contributors may be called the *achievers*. Other, more tradition-oriented groups overemphasize the status of the *inheritors*, persons to whom status is accorded because of their family connections, inherited wealth, professional roles, or distinctions that are highly regarded in our society. Successful businessmen, politicians in high office, sports heroes, and sometimes doctors, ministers, and professors are granted high status of this kind even when their actual contributions to a group are minimal. They are listened to with respect although their suggestions may frustrate, rather than help, group objectives.

Different groups place different emphases on the roles played by achievers as compared with inheritors. A major block to planned change may be that the inheritors, who lack the specific capabilities needed by the group, are allowed to monopolize leadership roles or even have these roles thrust upon them in some situations. Generally these inheritors not only frustrate change efforts but successfully block the development of leadership capabilities in those who have the skills, knowledge, and understanding so desperately needed by the group.

Groups also differ in their manner of handling power. In some cases effective power rests on authority, on the right to control others, which derives from the group itself and is attached to certain roles such as president or chairman. In other cases it may rest on influence, that is, on the ability, possessed by most achievers, to control others through individual competence. In groups that operate formally, the power of authority may be so great that the power of influence cannot be exerted. The designated leader may deal so authoritatively with the group that no other leadership has a chance to express itself. In less formal groups, on the other hand, while the power of influence may be so overwhelming that the designated chairman becomes only a figurehead, he may also be freed to concentrate entirely on the democratic functioning of the group.

PERSONALITY AND THE GROUP

Two variables help explain why groups with identical organizations and purposes can behave so differently: individual personalities in the groups and the working climate that they determine.

Personality is a product of an individual's exposure to group relationships in his formative years. It consists of attitudes about himself and the behavior he has acquired from the groups he has been most fully exposed to, particularly his family. It is the result of the interaction between constitutional endowments, such as physical make-up, health, looks, temperament, and capacities, and the degree of satisfaction of an individual's psychological needs in his present and past group relationships.

Since the family is the group to which individuals normally make their first and most fundamental adjustments, it has priority in the shaping of personality. But where the family fails to fulfill its functions, as in broken-home situations, other groups or individuals may play a determining role. Their success in shaping a personality will depend primarily on the degree of intimacy they can maintain with the individual and, hence, on how they satisfy his psychological needs.

PERSONALITY CHANGE

When individuals move from one community to another, they generally identify themselves with new groups that are like the ones they left, particularly in regard to socioeconomic status, educational level, and religious and political attitudes. These groups often have the same standards of operation and put much the same value on achievers versus inheritors as did their counterparts in the original community. Consequently, individuals will fit into the new groups without having to make noticeable adjustments in their personality structures. For this reason young people, although they may have acquired a great deal of knowledge, competence, and maturity from four years of college, often will not show appreciable changes in their basic personalities. Some exceptions may be found among young persons from farming communities with limited social opportunities who have had to adjust to predominantly urban norms at college, or other young people from limited backgrounds who, because of exceptional intelligence or athletic accomplishments, win scholarships to "Ivy League" schools and have to adjust to a social world of privilege quite unlike their own. In such cases their personalities may undergo changes for better or worse, depending on the encouragement or restraint they get from their new social groups.

When people are forced into situations where they have little or no choice of associates, the differences between them and the other members of the groups that they become a part of will make some changes in their personalities probable. Sometimes young people of middle-class backgrounds who have undertaken summer job experiences working with less fortunate boys and girls from ghetto neighborhoods have had to make serious adjustments in their personalities in order to cope with their duties. Any inherent sense of superiority they might feel because of their family backgrounds could be badly shaken by the negative reactions they get from their new underprivileged friends. These latter may despise them for being "softies" and demand that they show some real capabilities. If they have nothing to offer or are unwilling to make the effort, they may find themselves relegated to an inferior status in the group with very real consequences for their ability to do their jobs. On the other hand, if by their efforts they gain acceptance, they may, when they return to their homes, have a greater respect for the abilities of others and a deeper confidence in themselves, based on their new-found capabilities.

In the same way we may see marked changes in the personalities of shy youngsters under unusual circumstances. Take for example the teen-ager who, because he felt unwelcome in playground activities, secluded himself instead and doodled. It was not until one of his teachers discovered that his doodling revealed a marked skill at caricaturing and encouraged the boy to become the cartoonist of the school paper that the budding artist acquired esteem among his fellows that resulted in his gaining confidence in himself and overcoming his shyness.

Each group that the individual has to adjust to affects the way he looks at, thinks of, and feels about himself and the situations around him. As he carries these perceptions, thoughts, and feelings into new groups, he affects the tone and behavior of those groups.

PERSONALITY AND COMPETENCE

The images that people have of themselves—their personalities—do not always reflect their real competence in any field. Many people with unique capabilities habitually hide them under a mask of shyness or modesty. Others with complete confidence in themselves may totally lack real competence in any area. Because these are often the ones who put themselves forward, they are frequently chosen as leaders, often to the detriment of the group. Still others may be so domineering that they build up resistance in others and never really get a chance to prove that they can make a contribution to the group. Many such individuals—and they can make up a good proportion of every group—need help before they can be truly effective in group activities.

PERSONALITY GROWTH AS AN
OBJECTIVE OF PLANNED CHANGE

If community groups are to gain maximum benefit from change efforts, in the future as well as the present, the process by which they work out solutions to problems should allow for the personality fulfillment of every individual involved. Those who are shy should be freed of the pressures that inhibit their full participation in group decision making, and the dominating should be helped to feel greater appreciation for the contributions of others. Such transformations can be accomplished through training, and this training should be preliminary to any major effort in planned change at the community level.

When individuals begin to feel, perhaps for the first time, that they are accepted by others, that their opinions are important to the group, that whatever skills they have are wanted and needed to achieve group objectives, they will feel part of something really significant and worthy of their fullest support. The experience will be so satisfying to them that they will seek other opportunities for working with their fellows and they will not, as so often happens, have to be dragged into taking part in community-wide improvement efforts.

SUBMERGING THE INDIVIDUAL IN THE GROUP

Much resistance to involvement in group activity for planned change is based on a fear of losing one's identity in the group. And, of course, in recent years we have seen people swallowed up in communist or fascist types of organizations abroad or even extremist groups here at home. What is overlooked is that these are all authoritarian groups in which a condition of membership is giving up the right to think for oneself.

In all our relationships we are torn between satisfying our psychological needs within and through the groups of which we are a part and our desire for freedom of action. When we suppress the latter, we deny our right to think for ourselves, we suppress our creative capacities, and leave our critical faculties undeveloped. We become conformists or organization men. When, on the other hand, we treasure our individual freedom above the good opinion of the group, we alienate ourselves from our fellow members and may be rejected by them. A healthy development of the personalities of all members requires a balanced tension between individual freedom and the satisfaction of psychological needs within the group. Because not many community groups are in a position to provide this essential balance in their activities, they either drift toward authoritarian procedures on the one hand or ineffectiveness on the other.

The group needs the freedom-loving individual constantly to question attitudes, values, behavior patterns, and operating procedures, or the group can become static and unproductive and will not make the adjustments called for by a constantly changing social order. Mature, democratic groups welcome expressions of individual dissent because they recognize that only by permitting such freedom can both individual and group growth take place. The cohesiveness that develops from the satisfaction of psychological needs by all group members insures that whatever new norms or goals are established will be in the interest of all and will be supported by the group.

THE WASTE OF HUMAN RESOURCES

We are often told that the greatest waste in America today is the waste of human resources. This is usually interpreted to mean that thousands of men and women, often through no fault of their own, fail to develop the abilities they possess that could provide them with satisfying and productive lives. This is only a small part of the waste. Other thousands of men and women of proven ability are unable to make contributions to solving community problems because of their own, or somebody else's, personality hangups. Either their own shyness keeps them from taking their rightful place in community decision making, or the domineering, self-serving, nitpicking, or obstructive mannerisms of others make such participation impossible, no matter how great the community need may be. Avoiding this kind of waste of human resources ought to be given first consideration in every program of planned change.

REFERENCES AND READINGS

Batten, T. R. *The non-directive approach*. London: Oxford University Press, 1967.

Batten, T. R. *Communities and their development*. London: Oxford University Press, 1957.

Child, R. Utilizing community resources. *Journal of the Community Development Society*, 1974, Vol. 5, No. 2, 55-70.

Clinebell, H. D., Jr. *The people dynamic*. New York: Harper & Row, 1972.

Hollander, E. P., & Julian, J. W. Contemporary trends in the analysis of leadership processes. In H. C. Lindgren (Ed.), *Contemporary research in social psychology*. New York: John Wiley, 1973.

Reeves, E. T. *The dynamics of group behavior*. New York: American Management Association, 1970.

9

GROUP DECISION MAKING

GROUP SIZE

Numerous experiments show that individual practices and attitudes can be changed more effectively by working with small groups than by working with individuals separately. When the group as a whole accepts change, individuals tend to go along in order not to stand out.

A new idea or practice may be introduced to a community through a lecture or demonstration by an expert who presents the generally known facts and the reasons for recommending adoption. In such a setting, the individual listener cannot know precisely what the reaction of the other group members is and he can be easily misled. For example, applause, in response to an entertaining presentation, a humorous anecdote, or a pleasing personality, may hide strong resistance to the arguments presented. If the audience is divided into small groups after the lecture and asked to discuss the ideas that have been set forth, many of the individuals will go along with the apparent reaction of the total group.

There is no guarantee, of course, that any group, large or small, will favor the ideas presented in the lecture; this is the chance the lecturer and his sponsors have to take. In the long run, however, a negative response may be in their interest. Every exponent of change needs feedback from his audience in order to evaluate the ideas he is trying to present and his means of presenting them. There could be conditions that make his ideas unworkable in a particular locality, or he may have overlooked some general truths that need to be taken into consideration if his idea is to be regarded as sound. And there is always the possibility that he has left too many questions unanswered.

Audience reactions are valid only when they truly represent the thinking of all present. When they reflect only the biases of a vocal minority, they may be totally misleading. In groups of thirty-five to fifty people, two or three prominent individuals, with power, status, or vested interests to protect, can easily give the impression that the new idea presented by the lecturer is wholly unacceptable. The rest of the audience may, out of habit, fail to dispute the issue publicly, and the projected change never gets off the ground. On the other hand, these same influentials may favor the change because it is in their interest to do so, but in the end the unexpressed resistance of the rest of the audience will keep it from ever being implemented. This resistance could stem from a lack of information or explanations that the lecturer could have provided had he known they were needed.

If this same audience is divided into small discussion groups of half a dozen members each, the chances are much better that all present will express themselves and the two or three dominating individuals will affect only the groups they are assigned to. The other small groups will be able to think objectively and, when they report their decisions at the end of the discussion period, it will be evident where the majority of the people stand on the issue. Furthermore, dominating personalities frequently find the wind taken out of their sails when they do not have a sizeable audience to sway by their oratory.

LIMITATION OF TYPICAL
SMALL-GROUP PROCEDURES

Just dividing the audience into small discussion groups will not guarantee that everyone will participate, as enthusiasts for buzz-group procedures have often discovered.

The usual procedure for such small-group discussions is to appoint (or allow the group to choose) a leader and a recorder. If this does not result in good participation, the difficulty was probably one of two things, or a combination of both. First, the person picked as the leader dominated the group and failed to provide the climate in which other members could enter the conversation comfortably and enthusiastically. Few discussion leaders can resist the urge to see that their groups get results. They assume that this is expected of them, and they fulfill their responsibility by pushing the group and having something to say on every point. In doing so, of course, they cut off opportunities for others to participate. Second, the recorder, although perhaps the most conscientious one in the world, came up with a report that only vaguely resembled what the other group members thought they said. This is understandable as no two people hear exactly the same thing in any group session. Everyone hears selectively, or at least remembers selectively. Members ignore what seems unimportant to them or overlook what is said by people for whom they have limited respect or affection. When group members cannot see what is being recorded while the discussion is in progress, there is bound to be a discrepancy between what the recorder reports the group said and what the members think they said or agreed on. This often causes some group members to reject the process and the results as well.

Both these limitations can be overcome if the roles of the leader and of the reporter are combined in one person assigned to be a group facilitator. If the procedure is thoroughly explained before the small-group sessions begin, each group can pick its own facilitator and see that he follows the proper procedures. In protracted meetings, where a series of small-group sessions are contemplated, members can take turns playing the facilitator role. By doing so they become better group members because they learn to listen more to others rather than always trying to get their own ideas across.

HOW A GROUP FACILITATOR OPERATES

Each group, preferably of six people, should be seated around a table. One end of the table should be placed within about three feet of a blank wall space. A sheet of newsprint is hung on the wall with masking tape and on this the facilitator writes those points on which the group agrees. He should be provided with a grease pencil or felt-tipped pen so that every member of the group can see what he writes without difficulty. (If he uses a felt-tipped pen he will need an extra sheet of newsprint underneath the first so that the ink will not soak through and mar the wall.) The space between the table and the wall should be free of obstruction so that the facilitator can move about freely while writing on the newsprint, and, at the same time, keep in touch with the discussion as it proceeds. He should be on his feet and prepared to write as soon as the group assembles.

It is important that the facilitator see his role as quite different from that of the typical discussion leader and to this end he should observe certain rules of procedure.

1. *He listens.*

   He should not be afraid of silence. As long as the facilitator keeps from talking, the others can think. Eventually someone will become frustrated by silence and start the ball rolling.

2. *He gets agreement on the group's task.*

   No matter how simple the group assignment may be, the facilitator should insist that members state it in their own words so that there is no possibility of misunderstanding. This is a very good way to get them to loosen up and begin expressing themselves.

3. *When necessary he restates for accuracy ideas suggested by others.*
   He makes sure that the originator of the idea agrees with the restatement of the remark.

4. *If an idea meets with general approval of the group, at least tentatively, he writes it on the newsprint.*

5. *As new ideas are presented and accepted, he checks them for consistency with what is already on the newsprint.*
   Group thinking differs from individual thinking in that it has access to more data. As this information becomes available in the discussion the group may well want to change its course or even reverse itself.

6. *If he has ideas of his own, he presents them in a tentative manner for the group members to evaluate as they evaluate one another's ideas.*
   He uses expressions such as "Does this fit in here?" or "Is this what we are trying to say?" or "Do you agree with this?" The facilitator should let the rest of the group express itself first and participate only sparingly himself lest he keep others from taking part freely and confidently.

7. *He listens. This is the hardest job of all.*[1]

When the group has finished its discussion, the ideas that have been accepted are on the newsprint. If there are words crossed out, phrases added, or evidence of other changes, the members have been doing good group thinking. A word-perfect report often means a one-man job with a minimum of interplay between members.

When all the groups are called together in joint session, each facilitator brings his sheet of newsprint, hangs it with the others, and presents his report with a minimum of explanation or elaboration. If all the groups have been working on the same task, the moderator of the joint session can combine them into one report. If each group had a separate task, the reports can very readily be pulled together in their proper sequence.

THE GROUP FACILITATOR
APPROACH TO SHARED LEADERSHIP

When a facilitator has learned to play his role properly he has become a democratic leader in the fullest sense and is less concerned about the

---

[1]For a useful method of developing listening skills, see Appendix III.

task and more concerned with the operating process of the group. He allows members the fullest opportunity to perform the leadership functions they are prepared to perform. As a result, their involvement is complete, and they will accept full responsibility for the group product.

Those who are responsible for organizing community problem-solving efforts should recognize that an effective means of training people to become democratic leaders is to give them practice in being group facilitators. In a problem-solving workshop, for example, different members should be chosen as facilitators for each step in the process. On such occasions it is good to start the workshop by explaining the role of the facilitator and putting the list of instructions for his role where it can be seen by all the groups. Each group should be instructed to see that its facilitator is not allowed to dominate the group. When all have had the opportunity to play the facilitator role, they will have a better appreciation of what it means to be a democratic leader, and they will be far more effective group members.

TRAINING FACILITATORS FOR WORKSHOPS

Occasionally community problem-solving workshops include people who do not respond favorably to the idea of undergoing training, or the time element might preclude such training. In such cases it will pay to have trained individuals on hand to act as facilitators for different discussion groups.

The training is relatively simple. Each trainee seeks to get his fellow trainees to agree on a topic to discuss and then guides them through the discussion according to the instructions for facilitators. After all the trainees have had an opportunity to play the role of facilitator, they should evaluate one another's performance. Two or three such training sessions with the same trainees may be desirable to give them the confidence that the method really works and that they are qualified to do the job.

GROUP ACCEPTANCE OF CHANGE

The use of facilitators can evoke maximum individual participation in group discussion. When this procedure is used as a follow-up to a lecture on individual, organizational, or community problems, the chances are that the lecture will provoke thought and, in time, stimulate action. Without such follow-up, the lecture may prove to be little more than entertainment and will not be evaluated for the ideas presented.

Many people resist getting involved in a discussion of certain so-called community problems because, as they see it, the issue as stated is not a problem at all, but someone's pet solution for which their support is being solicited. Or, if they do participate, it may be because they have strong feelings of opposition, which they are determined to air. Rural residents, for example, may respond in this way to proposals for rural zoning. Instead, if they were asked at the start to consider some of the community problems that affect them and to help decide what to do about them, they eventually would recognize the need for some kind of community controls, whatever form these might take.

We can define a problem as *a condition that has to be removed if the needs and satisfactions of the group as a whole are to be met.* It is something that must be changed, or done away with, before achieving conditions that are satisfactory to all.

In the light of this definition, such things as education, employment, housing, transportation, or recreation are not problems because, as they are stated, they are not conditions that require change. The related conditions that do need to be changed are poor education, underemployment or unemployment, substandard housing, inadequate public transportation, and lack of recreation. Such things as poverty, crime, delinquency, drug abuse, alcoholism, and vandalism all qualify as problems needing consideration, even though some of them may be symptoms of problems, rather than genuine problems. But by following the steps in the logical problem-solving process, community leaders arrive eventually at the underlying problem.

By failing to start with a real problem, many groups never find the best solution to their difficulty. For example, a church grown to the point where its existing facilities are inadequate to carry on its scheduled Christian education program may too readily see building a new Christian education facility as its problem. This could require a financial outlay that the congregation is unwilling or unable to undertake. Moreover, the church has not considered some alternative solutions that have been tried successfully in progressive, economy-minded churches throughout the country. These churches, instead of scheduling all their Christian education classes at ten o'clock on Sunday morning, set them at different hours during the week for different age groups. Thus they not only overcome the problem of limited classroom facilities, but provide greater flexibility in staffing and increase the attendance of teen-agers on Friday evening when a much-needed and healthy recreation program can be added as a follow-up to the Bible study class.

GROUP DECISION-MAKING PROCEDURES

Many groups find that decision making itself is a relatively easy matter. Their members are highly civilized people capable of carrying on well-mannered discussions with a minimum of disagreement or surface friction. But their decisions are never implemented and seldom is anything changed. They have fallen into the rut of respectability and have failed to recognize that implementing decisions is an integral part of the decision-making process. Airing differences of opinion and presenting alternative points of view are constructive parts of this process. If they are stifled merely for the sake of appearances, surface agreement will not be followed by the support required for implementation.

There are two different approaches that can be used for dealing with group problem solving and decision making. Both procedures aim less at achieving ideal solutions to the problem at hand than at getting the broadest possible support for whatever solutions are agreed upon. One approach is usually called the Group Decision-Making Process and the other the Logical Problem-Solving Process. In both cases, of course, the use of small discussion groups and of group facilitators is imperative. The first approach can be used when the problem is a fairly clear-cut one with limited ramifications.

Following are the steps in the Group Decision-Making Process.

1. *Define the problem.*

   Make sure that it is a genuine problem, according to the definition provided earlier, and then state it clearly and precisely. For example, both a "housing shortage" and a "lack of transportation" are inadequate as descriptions. They would be more meaningful if stated as a "shortage of housing for low-income families" or a "lack of cheap, fast public transportation."

2. *List all possible alternative solutions, but do not immediately evaluate them.*

   The chairman should insist that the group produce half a dozen or more solutions to avoid being saddled with an undesirable one from a member who has more status than know-how but who often dominates community decisions.

   If members of the group can propose as many alternatives as they want, without feeling that they have to defend them, then the group can make maximum use of the imagination that is available. If necessary, "brainstorming" may be resorted to. For example, the group can consider what it would do if the organization were given a million dollars to solve its problem. A careful consideration of the solutions arrived at in this way might reveal that at least one or two, with minor changes, could be attempted without having to depend on contributions from outside.

3. *Weigh all alternatives in terms of the consequences, both good and bad.*

    If the bad consequences clearly outweigh the good, that particular solution can be eliminated from the list, or it can be left in for later comparison with the other possible solutions. By carrying out this step as objectively as possible, the group can begin to divorce each alternative from the individual or faction that recommended it and place the merits of each alternative above personal or factional considerations.

4. *Determine what each remaining alternative would require from members of the decision-making group.*

    This is a means of finding out whether individuals in the decision-making group are prepared to do their share in accomplishing a given solution or whether they expect to pass that responsibility on to somebody else. Will it require a fifty-dollar contribution from each member, twenty hours of footwork on everyone's part, or contributions of food, clothing, materials, or other needed supplies? If each member is not ready to do all that is required of him, he cannot "pass the buck" to others or to another committee. Some solutions will be eliminated by the time this step has been completed.

5. *Choose the solution gaining most support.*

    If the previous steps have been conscientiously carried out by the group, the merits of one solution over the rest should begin to be apparent by the time the fifth step is reached. The chairman then has only to ask for an expression of agreement on this particular solution, making sure, of course, that anyone opposed is still free to express himself.

    In organizations where a recorded vote is required by the constitution, the vote should be taken only as a formality after the decision has been reached in the manner described above.

6. *Organize for carrying out the decision.*

    Individual assignments for action need to be made and accepted and subgroups appointed to handle specific aspects of the solution. More than one meeting may be required to take the group through the first five steps. Once a solution has been decided upon, however, it is well to get organized as soon as possible to carry it out. This may mean gathering information on which further action will depend.

7. *Provide for a later evaluation of the results of the decision.*

    The continued effectiveness of the problem-solving group may depend on how well this job is done. In some groups, the goal members set for themselves is so vague or is stated in such imprecise language that they will never know whether or not they have accomplished it. They need to ask, "How will we know at the end of the year how close we have come to reaching our goal?" If this question cannot be answered readily, a more measurable goal should be chosen.

Every group must occasionally have a sense of accomplishment if it is to remain effective. If, for example, the goal is to build a community center costing $30,000, it would be best to consider this a long-range goal and set a smaller amount of money as a goal for the current year. When that amount is raised, the sense of accomplishment will spur the group on to complete the long-range goal.

BLOCKS TO GROUP DECISION MAKING

Most people fear the consequences of any step that goes beyond their own limited experience. However, when others can demonstrate that, through the proper use of the decision-making process, other ways of doing things have been known to get results, people are willing to go along with them.

Everyone brings to each situation his own prior loyalties to other groups and individuals. But when decision-making procedures are working properly, and individuals become absorbed with others in getting alternative solutions into the open and then list for each as many good or bad consequences as they can think of, it becomes increasingly difficult to remember who was the originator of any one alternative. Each is seen in terms of its own merits or limitations.

Members of the decision-making group need to be free to act as they think best and not be bound to speak for the separate community organizations that each happens to represent. This gives them the freedom to make sound decisions that they then will be proud to take back to their respective organizations for support. If they lack this freedom, decisions will satisfy neither them nor their organizations.

Parliamentary procedures are intended for situations in which opposing groups are often more interested in power plays than in sound decisions. Less formal procedures are much more appropriate for community groups; they get better results, and they relieve group tensions.

MAKING MAXIMUM USE
OF SMALL-GROUP SESSIONS

At any point in the decision-making process, small discussion groups under the guidance of their respective facilitators can work on the same step together. When they have completed each step, they can consolidate their results. Or they can be asked to undertake special assignments. For example, if a number of alternative solutions have been suggested as a result of step 2, each group can take a different one and, in step 3, propose as many good and bad consequences as it can think of. When each facilitator has finished giving his report to the total group, he should ask if the group as a whole can think of any consequences that have been overlooked. If any are mentioned, he can add them to his report. In this way maximum results can be obtained within a given period of time while still achieving the maximum involvement of all group members in the whole process.

REFERENCES AND READINGS

Drucker, P. F. *The effective executive*. New York: Harper & Row, 1966.

Dubey, S. N. Community action programs and citizen participation. In G. Zaltman, P. Kotler, & I. Kaufman (Eds.), *Creating social change*. New York: Holt, Rinehart & Winston, 1972.

Petelle, J. L. The role of conflict in decision. In R. S. Cathcart & L. A. Samovar (Eds.), *Small group communication*. Dubuque, Iowa: Wm. C. Brown, 1970.

Strauss, B., & Strauss, F. *New ways to better meetings*. New York: The Viking Press, 1964.

10

THE LOGICAL PROBLEM-SOLVING PROCESS

Although the group decision-making method discussed in the last chapter is useful in dealing with fairly concrete problems, many "people" problems require a different approach. Often what the community perceives may not be a basic problem, but only a symptom of one. Such so-called "problems" as juvenile delinquency, school dropouts, and drug abuse fall into this category. However, it is neither necessary nor desirable to try to persuade people that what they are concerned about it not a fundamental issue. To maintain their interest and involvement, it is best to accept the problem as they see it and proceed from there.

The Logical Problem-Solving Process achieves this and yet gets at the basic problems. It also makes it possible for people to discover for themselves that there is seldom one simple cause for community problems. For example, those who too readily blame school dropouts on indifferent parents can learn that there are many other reasons for youngsters to drop out of school.

THE EXPLORATORY GROUP

The great weakness of many problem-solving groups is that they try to move ahead too fast. They have solutions in hand before they have properly identified the problem, or they try to involve important and busy people before they can clearly convey what difficulty they are trying to cope with.

Here an exploratory committee can be very helpful. As few as half a dozen interested individuals can take the preliminary steps in the problem-solving process before the community at large is involved. This exploratory group need not have a fixed membership. From time to time it can include individuals who have access to important information but who may not be able or willing to stay with the group once they have made their special contribution. And it may need to meet frequently over a period of weeks before it is ready to involve any appreciable number of people.

The exploratory group's deliberations should be tentative, subject to change from session to session as new information is added and as new individuals react to the matter in hand, so that it maintains a high degree of flexibility.

In one of our major East Coast metropolitan areas, for example, a small exploratory group started to tackle the problem of unemployment, as it was defined by the state employment commission. Over a period of weeks representatives of welfare departments and community-action programs and other individuals with close ties to poverty neighborhoods were invited to help define the problem. On the basis of their testimony the problem was eventually seen not as unemployment, since only a few people were actually without jobs of any kind, but as underemployment. As the dimensions of the total problem became apparent, it seemed wise to limit the group's consideration to the underemployment of the hard-core poor, 16 to 21 years of age, within one political unit of the metropolitan area. With this statement of the problem in hand, the exploratory group had little difficulty in recruiting the help of a wide variety of civic leaders in setting up a full-scale problem-solving seminar.

THE STEPS IN THE PROBLEM-SOLVING PROCESS

There are five major steps in the problem-solving process. In a first phase the exploratory group should complete steps one and two in preparation for the second phase, a seminar to which a much larger group of representative citizens should be invited. These latter should be asked to react to what the exploratory group agreed upon and to make any additions or changes that they think necessary.

Exploratory Group Phase

1. *Define the problem and set the limits within which the group wants to work.*

   There must be agreement on the terms used in the statement of the problem. In the case of the school dropout problem, for example, it is essential to distinguish between a genuine "dropout" and someone who is not attending school for a number of reasons beyond his control. If he lacks the required physical or mental capabilities, is he a dropout? If he is of school age but is undergoing on-the-job training in a factory or professional organization, is he considered a dropout? If the answer is "no" to both questions, how is a dropout to be defined to exclude these individuals?

The exploratory group also needs to define the limits within which it wants to work. The school dropout problem might be limited to those boys who dropped out of elementary school in a given neighborhood or to both boys and girls in the entire public school system of the city who dropped out before completing high school. It is up to the group itself to determine what it wants the limits to be.

2. *List the situations that need to be changed if the problem is to be overcome.*

To make sure that no situations are overlooked it may be well in some cases to begin with broad categories of situations related to the problem. In the school-dropout example, there would be some situations having to do with the potential dropout's family, his peer groups in school (the extracurricular activity groups), his peer groups outside of school (the gangs), the school system itself and what it has to offer, and, finally, the community in which he lives. In the example of the under-employment of hard-core poor, there would be the home situations of the youths, their experiences in getting and holding jobs, employer and union attitudes toward them, and so on.

When the exploratory group has completed step two, it can arrange under various headings the several situations identified. In the job problem the situations that need to be changed can be put into the following categories: health, financial problems, day-care needs, transportation, preliminary counseling, job counseling, job training, and jobs now (making new jobs available).

Problem-solving Seminar Phase

The exploratory group should now organize a full day's problem-solving seminar. A date should be set for an all-day meeting and a large, all-purpose hall picked for the problem-solving seminar. It should have plenty of chairs and tables and blank wall space on which to post newsprint.

Task forces of six to a dozen people should be set up to tackle each of the categories of situations to be changed, such as those listed previously for the underemployment problem. The committee should develop a roster of organizations, agencies, and individuals to be included in each task force. As far as possible, status figures should be avoided; only those individuals who are most likely to give the time and effort to get the job done should be chosen.

Individual members of the exploratory committee should telephone those who are to be invited to participate on each of the task forces. Top executives of business organizations and some agencies should be asked to assign some of their qualified individuals to participate, but the invitations, when they are sent, should go by name to the individuals who are expected to attend.

Each task force should carefully review the original problem and the situation it deals with to make sure that there is agreement with the exploratory group decisions. If there is not, the members of the task force should restate the situation as they see it and be prepared to explain the change. Then they should take up the next step in the logical problem-solving process.

3. *Establish a goal for the situation.*

As used here, a "goal" is simply a statement of what the group thinks the situation should be. In the school dropout problem some of the task force goals might be that no student should be prevented from completing his high school education because of lack of finances or that the high school curriculum should meet the generalized needs of all non-college-bound as well as college-bound students in the city. In the statement of a goal no attempt is to be made to indicate a solution. That is a matter for later concern. The most meaningful goals are those that are measurable so that after a given length of time it can be determined whether or not they are being accomplished and to what degree.

4. *Identify the obstacles that need to be overcome in order to achieve each goal.*

The primary purpose of this step is to discover the target group or groups for the task force's action program. Is it to be the general public, special categories of citizens, institutional administrators, or local governing bodies? Identifying these target groups and assuming what their opposition, if any, is likely to be will tell something about what needs to be done and in what order. For example, many employers and labor unions resist hiring hard-core poor youth and must be convinced that their self-interest lies in putting them on a payroll and keeping them off the street.

5. *Recommend the best course of action to achieve the goal with the designated target group or groups in mind.*

This should include a statement of the task to be undertaken and a deadline for achieving each step in it, qualitative and quantitative measures of how well the job is to be done, and the assignment of responsibilities for the accomplishment of each task.

For example, in its attempt to broaden the high school curriculum to meet the needs of the non-college-bound student, the task force may recognize that it requires more information about what those needs are. The task force's action plan may consist of the following preliminary steps.

- Hold an evening meeting with a representative group of school dropouts to get an expression of what they feel they lack to make a more successful adjustment to the workaday world. Both employed and unemployed dropouts are to be invited to participate as well as members of the school administration. Two task force members will make the arrangements and act as group facilitators.

- To another meeting invite personnel managers and other representatives of firms that employ young people to discover the generalized skills and attitudes that employers find essential.

- Hold a third meeting of health and welfare agency representatives, juvenile court officials, and other qualified individuals who can help identify what these young people need to make better adjustments in their homes and in their neighborhood relationships.

- Bring together the task force members and school administrative officers who attended the first three steps to consolidate the findings of the three sessions and determine what adjustments can be made in the school curriculum to meet the needs of these young people.

For each of these steps different members of the task force should be asked to undertake the responsibility of inviting the participants and making whatever other arrangements are necessary.

Closing the Seminar

About an hour before the problem-solving seminar is scheduled to close, all the task forces should be called together in joint session. They should be seated so that they can see the sheets of newsprint containing the task force reports. Each group facilitator is called on to read his report in turn.

The seminar chairman should encourage all present to react to each report, make suggestions for changes, or provide pertinent information that the task forces have missed. Such information should be added to the reports if it meets with general approval.

The chairman should instruct each facilitator to edit his report, put it into a brief outline, and return it to the seminar committee with the names of those who participated. The committee can then consolidate the reports into a final document, duplicate it, and have it distributed to all participants.

The members of the joint session should decide to whom the report should be sent for possible further action. In the meantime the separate task forces should continue with whatever steps they had selected and should keep the committee informed of such action so that at the end of an agreed-upon period there can be a progress report.

The seminar committee should make every attempt to secure the widest publicity for its reports through the mass media, but more particularly it should encourage seminar participants to report their activity to the community-minded organizations they belong to. Discussion of the reports by these organizations will foster attitudes favorable to the recommended changes.

CRITERIA FOR SUCCESSFUL PROBLEM-SOLVING OPERATIONS

The success of any problem-solving seminar that attempts to follow these steps will depend on:

1. whether the exploratory committee has laid the groundwork so that all who attend the seminar will have confidence from the start that they are undertaking, in a businesslike manner, something that merits their concern;

2. whether various points of view that are relevant to the problem at hand are represented;

3. whether representatives are included from other community-minded organizations whose support will be essential to carrying out whatever goals are agreed upon; and finally,

4. whether the small discussion groups allow free give-and-take so that all involved can make their maximum contribution to the discussions.

The basic purpose of the logical problem-solving process is not just to arrive at a solution on paper but to gain the broadest possible community support for the decisions made, so that implementation can be assured.

REFERENCES AND READINGS

Napier, R. W., & Gershenfeld, M. K. *Groups: Theory and experience*. Boston: Houghton Mifflin, 1973.

Thelen, H., & Dickerson, W. The growth of the group. In W. K. Bennis, K. D. Benne, & R. Chin (Eds.), *The planning of change*. New York: Holt, Rinehart & Winston, 1962.

11
THE TRAINING OF COMMUNITY LEADERS

The citizens who have the greatest impact on change efforts are those who have demonstrated that they are change-oriented through their membership in organizations with community improvement goals. When these individuals are also recognized leaders of their organizations, they will probably have member support for whatever decisions they are involved in making.

Yet most leaders see the community as an extension of their respective groups instead of in its overall aspects. For them the community is the chamber of commerce community, the Jaycee community, the PTA, League of Women Voters, civic federation, or Presbyterian Church community. For this reason it is often hard to involve them in efforts at planned change for the total community. This also explains why there is so much overlapping and duplication of effort by these organizations, as well as an amazing lack of communication among them.

Nevertheless, within their respective organizations, most leaders are seeking solutions to serious problems such as member apathy, indifference, poor attendance, and poor support for organization goals. Starting with these felt needs of leaders, a training program can be set up, preferably at the county level, which can increase citizen involvement and greatly facilitate the achievement of change objectives. The training should consist of a day-and-a-half workshop in logical problem solving and effective group techniques.

SETTING UP A WORKSHOP
STEERING COMMITTEE

The change agent may be working in a county with a number of towns and villages as well as open-country residents, or in a major political unit of a metropolis that contains suburban areas and neighborhoods. In either case he will want to bring together a dozen people representing all segments of the community and as many different community-minded groups as possible. "Community-minded" indicates those organizations, including churches, that are concerned about their community, as distinct from other perfectly legitimate organizations such as bowling teams, country clubs, and social clubs, which primarily serve the individual needs of their members.

At this gathering the change agent will explain the purpose of a workshop in logical problem solving and effective group techniques and suggest that each community-minded organization send to such a workshop two or three of its leaders who may be expected to hold office in the coming year. The workshop is intended to help them plan their organizational programs to avoid the problems that have been accumulating over the years.

If the steering committee members respond enthusiastically to the idea of such a training program, their first job will be to identify the community-minded organizations in their respective political units that should be invited to participate. If lists are not immediately available, committee members should be asked to mail or telephone them to the change agent.

The day-and-a-half workshop program will require an evening session, from 7:30 to 10 p.m., on one day, and another session from 9 a.m. until 3 p.m. the following day. To meet the work schedules of the people invited, both a midweek workshop (say, Tuesday and Wednesday) and a weekend workshop (Friday night and Saturday) should be scheduled.

Depending on the facilities available, sixty participants should be considered the maximum number in any one workshop, although thirty would be closer to the ideal. Invitations sent out should include two or three return cards to be filled out by those who are willing to commit themselves to attending full time. When sixty people have signed up for either workshop, the registration for that workshop should be closed.

LOCATION OF THE WORKSHOP

The steering committee will want a central location with ample parking space. They should look for a building with a large all-purpose room that has plenty of movable tables and chairs and suitable restroom facilities. If sixty people are expected to attend there should be room to set up ten tables, each near a blank wall space on which newsprint can be hung for the facilitators' use. Also there should be a place at one end of the room where all sixty can sit together for the joint sessions at which discussion group reports will be made and basic theory presented. Such facilities are often found in elementary and high school cafeterias and gymnasiums, National Guard armories, church parish houses, and community centers. (See Figure 11.1.)

Strange as it may seem, holding the entire workshop in one large room has more advantages than disadvantages. When two or more rooms are used, unless they are immediately adjoining, valuable time is lost in frequent moving from small groups to joint sessions. And when all the discussion groups are in session together in one room they tend to pace each other and set general standards of operation.

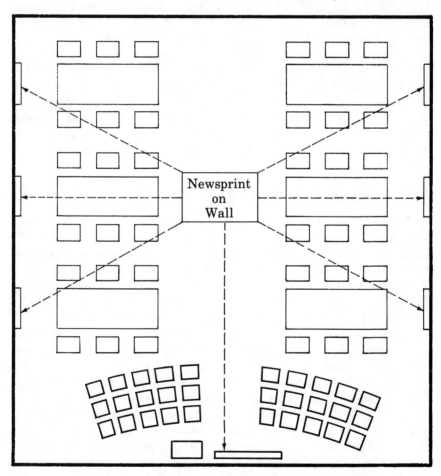

Figure 11.1.   The Ideal Workshop Arrangement for
Thirty Participants

WORKSHOP SPONSORSHIP

Regardless of the change agent's own professional identification, great care should be taken not to identify the workshop program too closely with any one agency. The names of the members of the steering committee and the organizations they represent may suffice to indicate broad community support.

Since the second day of the workshop will run from nine in the morning until three in the afternoon, some provision will have to be made for lunch. If the participants disperse and eat wherever they choose, valuable time will be lost. But if they stay together during the lunch hour, they will have an excellent opportunity for getting acquainted and communicating their concerns. In most communities box lunches can be sent in from a local restaurant or caterer.

Since it is desirable to provide coffee breaks in the morning and evening, the price of the coffee should be added to the cost of each box lunch. The total can be the workshop registration fee, which should be requested in the letter of invitation. This is important. People are much more prone to honor a commitment when they have invested something in it, no matter how little, than when there is no financial obligation involved. But the fee should not be a barrier to individuals with limited means.

THE WORKSHOP PROGRAM

It should be noted in the invitation that the workshop program will consist of alternating small-group and joint sessions. The former will apply the steps in the logical problem-solving process to a demonstration community problem and provide valuable practice in the skills needed to achieve maximum involvement in group decision making. The joint sessions will include reports from the small discussion groups as well as presentations on the principles of group motivation.

Many experts in group dynamics insist that a group should not be asked to deal with a problem that it has not selected itself. However, when individuals drawn from a variety of backgrounds make up a workshop, it is often difficult and time consuming to get them to agree on a common problem and they often settle on one they will find the answers to in the procedures used in the workshop. For that reason, it is preferable to use a problem that effectively illustrates the steps in the logical problem-solving process. The ideal problem for this purpose is the school dropout since, as it exists in most communities, leaders will be familiar with it. The problem of underemployment serves almost equally well.

During the theory sessions, the change agent will want to present the five areas of basic theory, covered in the following chapters of this book. If he has a good memory he may emphasize the major points of his presentations by writing them on a blackboard or on sheets of newsprint. He would particularly want to stress definition of terms since many of the participants will want to take notes on them.

However, writing while talking, which requires turning his back on his audience, will not only slow his delivery but interrupt the flow of the discussion. It would be much better if he could prepare materials ahead of time on hand-lettered charts or, best of all, on transparencies for use with an overhead projector. Lightweight, compact overhead projectors are now available which can be used in a fully lighted room so that the speaker always remains in full communication with his audience while projecting important parts of his message on the screen. The transparencies for these projectors can be typed or hand-lettered, are easy for the audience to read, can be illustrated if need be (occasionally spiced with humor), and can serve as an outline of the material to be covered.

OPENING THE WORKSHOP

Someone should be on hand to greet workshop participants as they arrive, see that they are properly registered, and provide each with a name tag. These tags should be filled out with a felt-tipped pen in letters large enough so that names can be read from a distance of ten or more feet. Tags can be prepared with names typed at the top, leaving enough room for the participants to write in the name by which they want to be called in the workshop.

The workshop coordinator, as the change agent should be known at this point, will ask the participants to gather in a joint session first. He will introduce himself and then ask each person present to give only his name, organization, and the locality from which he comes, no more.

The coordinator will then explain what the workshop is expected to accomplish and prepare the participants to begin working in small groups of six each. The best way to make sure that these are composed of people representing different organizations and localities is to have them number off. If there are thirty people present, there will be enough for five groups, so they will number off in fives. However, if there are far more men than women, or vice versa, the coordinator may find it desirable to have the men number off first and the women later so that the groups will be mixed. The same can be done when any minorities are present.

The coordinator will first point out the shortcomings of past small discussion group procedures and then present the list of instructions for the use of group facilitators. He will recommend that each group pick a new facilitator for each session so that a large number will have a chance to practice the role during the workshop sessions. He will indicate the sheets of newsprint and recommend that facilitators start writing group reactions on the newsprint just as soon as their groups assemble and get organized.

The coordinator will then present the definition of a problem, explain its significance, and suggest that the groups follow the steps in the logical problem-solving process to arrive at a solution to the school dropout problem. He will state what is involved in the first step in the process and caution them not to try to go beyond this step in their first session. He should remind them that their concern in the workshop is to learn the steps in the process and that, therefore, they will not be able to spend as much time on each step as would otherwise be the case. At this point he can suggest that each person go to the table identified with his number from the count-off.

The coordinator should circulate among the groups as unobtrusively as possible while they are in session, answering questions, if any are raised. He should encourage the facilitators to put ideas on the newsprint as soon as they are agreed upon. The tendency will be for facilitators to jot ideas on a piece of paper in anticipation of transferring them to the newsprint when they have completed their discussions, but this defeats the purpose of getting ideas up where all can see them.

The coordinator will have to determine for himself how much time to allow for these small-group sessions. Half to three-quarters of an hour should be enough. He does not need to wait until all have completed the first step and written it on the newsprint. Some groups will have wasted time in pointless chit-chat and others will want to copy on the newsprint what they have previously written out on paper. When they see what others have accomplished in the same period of time they will learn to adopt more efficient procedures.

The coordinator should call the groups back into joint session and ask the facilitators to hang their newsprint sheets on the wall or on easels in front of the combined groups. He will ask each facilitator to read the findings of his group without any elaboration or explanations. Then, in preparation for the next step, the coordinator can consolidate the findings in a statement that all can agree upon.

PROGRAM AGENDA SUMMARY

The entire workshop program should be as follows.

1. *Joint Session*
   a. Introductions
   b. Presentation—The Group Facilitator Role and Definition of a Problem

   Small Groups
   a. Step 1 in the Problem-Solving Process

2. *Joint Session*
   a. Group Reports
   b. Theory Presentation on Group Norms

   Small Groups
   a. Step Two in the Problem-Solving Process

3. *Joint Session*
   a. Group Reports
   b. Theory Presentation on Conformity Pressures

   Small Groups
   a. Step Three in the Problem-Solving Process

4. *Joint Session*
   a. Group Reports
   b. Theory Presentation on the Principles of Group Process

   Small Groups
   a. Step Four in the Problem-Solving Process

5. *Joint Session*
   a. Group Reports
   b. Theory Presentation on the Circular Process of Social Interaction

   Small Groups
   a. Step Five in the Problem-Solving Process

6. *Joint Session*
   a. Theory Session on New Concepts of Leadership

   Small Groups
   a. Workshop Evaluation

7. *Joint Session*
   a. Group Reports on Evaluation
   b. Workshop Summary

The coordinator will have to time the workshop by ear because no two groups will conduct themselves at the same pace, and the size of the total group will determine how much time is required for the group reports. In order for the members of the workshop to develop some kind of rapport before the first evening is over and be eager to return the next day, they should cover at least the second step in the logical problem-solving process that night. The next morning they can begin with the theory session on conformity pressures and break for lunch whenever it is convenient between sessions.

Because of the shortage of time, the coordinator may find it worthwhile to use a prepared transparency to illustrate step five of the logical problem-solving process. This makes it easier to get across to the participants the purpose of this step: to attain the whole-hearted support of those who would most likely oppose the goals of the decision-making group.

WORKSHOP EVALUATION

When the coordinator has completed the final theory session on new concepts of leadership and has allowed time for discussion, he should send the participants back to their small groups to evaluate the workshop. He can suggest that they separately consider the workshop as a whole, the role of the group facilitator, the theory sessions, the small-group discussions, and the logical problem-solving process. They can then use the following rating system with the accompanying numerical equivalents to arrive at an average score: Very Helpful (4), Helpful (3), Not Very Helpful (2), Not Helpful At All (1).

For each item evaluated, the number of raters should be multiplied by the score for that response. The total for each item is then divided by the number of responses to get the average score. For example, four members of Group A may say the group facilitator's role was *very helpful* ($4 \times 4 = 16$), one *helpful* ($1 \times 3 = 3$), and one *not very helpful* ($1 \times 1 = 1$). The total of 20, divided by the number of responses (6) gives 3.3 for that item, or somewhere between helpful and very helpful.

When they have completed this numerical evaluation, the groups should be asked to complete the following statement: *The workshop would have been better if . . .*

The groups can then be called back into joint session to share their findings.

SHARING THE COORDINATOR'S ROLE

Even the most personable change agent will find that, however well he presents his theory materials and coordinates the small-group activities in his workshop, the job could have been done better by a team, even if their individual performances were not up to his. For example, one person could supervise all of the small-group activities while others present portions of the theory materials.

The change agent should thus try as early as possible to involve some of his associates—or, better still, some of the participants from his first workshop—in presenting different parts of the workshop program. After his first workshop the change agent may find that some of the organization leaders or agency representatives who participated are so taken with the workshop idea that they will want to help in future workshops and will be willing to undergo some special training sessions for this purpose. Their help should be encouraged. Graduate students who are preparing for careers as professional change agents can become valuable associates and help immeasurably in such workshop activities.

REFERENCES AND READINGS

Argyris, C. T-groups for organizational effectiveness. In G. Zaltman, P. Kotler, & I. Kaufman (Eds.), *Creating social change*. New York: Holt, Rinehart & Winston, 1972.

Batten, T. R. *The non-directive approach*. London: Oxford University Press, 1967.

Batten, T. R. *Communities and their development*. London: Oxford University Press, 1957.

Bradford, L. P. Membership in the t-group. In R. S. Cathcart & L. A. Samovar (Eds.), *Small group communication*. Dubuque: Wm. C. Brown, 1970.

Egan, G. *Face to face*. Monterey, Calif.: Brooks/Cole Publishing Co., 1973.

Fiedler, F. E., & Chemers, M. M. *Leadership and effective management*. Glenview, Ill.: Scott Foresman, 1974.

GROUP NORMS

Once the members of an organization have identified their problem, their next concern is with the norms of the people who in one way or another are involved in the problem. Some existing norms may make change difficult, but others can offer possibilities for constructive action. In either case the matter of norms deserves careful consideration.

Group norms are those attitudes, values, and forms of behavior that the group as a whole requires or expects of its members. All human groups, regardless of their size, composition, or length of existence, have norms even if they are never expressly stated by any member of the group. They may become evident only when tested.

In our definition *attitudes* are what people think or feel about things, their likes and dislikes, as well as their stand on political, religious, and controversial issues generally. We think of these attitudes as highly personal, but most can be traced back to the groups people have belonged to. Because of their attitudes people acquire such labels as liberal, conservative, fundamentalist, high church, strait-laced, teetotaler, libertine, egghead, hippie, and the like.

Values are those attitudes that people give top priority to at a given time and in particular situations. For example, thoughtfulness and sincerity may be of prime importance in choosing friends, but for selecting business associates or candidates for political office other values prevail. Some religious groups believe that more than an elementary education is dangerous. or sinful, communists subordinate personal freedom to party discipline, and many Americans today consider self-indulgence more important than good health. All of these are parts of value systems.

Forms of behavior include not only specific acts that people perform, but their manner of dress and speech, and their day-to-day habits. Like attitudes and values, they become a part of a person's make-up because of the influence different groups have over him. If a person's norms are contrary to those of his family, they may sometimes be traced to his peer groups, as is the case with hippie dress and hair styles.

By and large, people tend to identify with groups that have norms that are fairly consistent with their own. When circumstances force them to participate in a group with norms they do not agree with, they will generally make themselves as inconspicuous as possible to maintain good relationships with the members of the group. They will not express radical ideas in a conservative gathering, they will refrain from drinking in the company of nondrinkers, and they will ignore statements that conflict with the norms they have abided by in the past.

FORMATION OF GROUP NORMS

In a given society the dominant culture maintains certain generalized norms that are looked upon as characterizing the people of that society. Americans abroad are easily recognized by their clothes, their manner of speech, and by the attitudes that govern their relations with other people.

These same norms vary subtly from region to region within a society itself, yet they are distinct enough to provide a fairly clear image of the people involved. A New England Yankee, for example, is distinct from a Southerner or a Middle Westerner, although these differences may not always be recognizable to someone from abroad.

While communities within a region may share the norms of the larger area, they may also have norms of their own which characterize them as progressive, cooperative, smug, wide-open, or friendly. To professional workers from government or private agencies, these community norms often have a great deal to do with the success of programs they carry on in these areas.

Within a given community there is a wide assortment of formal and informal organizations, each with its own set of norms. These generally include some of the community and regional norms but have enough character of their own to distinguish them from one another. People often characterize each other by what organizations they belong to. While this is a form of stereotyping, it has some validity since people generally identify with those groups holding norms they agree with.

Even within organizations, informal groups or cliques maintain norms distinct from those of the parent organization. Churches may be split between high- and low-church factions, and social clubs are often divided between those who drink and those who do not, or those who play cards and those who prefer to dance or socialize in other ways.

THE FUNCTION OF NORMS

Norms provide individuals with ready-made ways of behaving or thinking that have been tested by man's accumulated experience. Without such norms man's decision-making powers would be taxed beyond endurance in his day-to-day activities.

As a rule, the older a culture, the more it relies on norms to determine individual behavior. In pre-communist China, for example, where Confucian norms permeated all levels of society for over 2,000 years, an individual's behavior was prescribed for him in almost every social situation and his responses became so automatic that he rarely thought of the original intent of any given norm.

Where there is a high degree of mobility, however, this effect may be offset by the influence of imported norms. For this reason old cities such as New York City that have high mobility will have fewer fixed norms than younger cities with less mobility.

NORMS AS A BASIS FOR
PREDICTING INDIVIDUAL BEHAVIOR

If one knows the groups that a person belongs to, one has a rough measure of what that person's attitudes, values, and forms of behavior are likely to be. This is, of course, much less true in a highly complex society such as ours than in a simpler society where individuals have fewer formal group relationships and, therefore, are more likely to have a consistent set of norms. But even in our highly urbanized culture we depend on a person's group relationships to tell us what we can expect from him in different situations. We assume he will be liberal or conservative, strait-laced or easygoing, tolerant or hypocritical depending on his associations.

ENFORCEMENT OF GROUP NORMS

Conformity to group norms is rewarded with praise and acceptance; nonconformity is punished with criticism and rejection. From earliest childhood every individual is trained to conform. Through punishment and rewards, his family teaches him the importance of thinking and behaving according to the norms it prescribes; later, his education continues the process. Consequently, he accepts such conformity pressures as natural and soon indulges his privilege of helping bring his peers in line with his own norms.

What is often overlooked is that these sanctions operate only upon members of the group holding the norms. They do not directly affect outsiders.

IMPORTANCE OF DIFFERENT TYPES OF NORMS

Attempts to bring about change often come to nothing because of the failure to recognize differences in norms at different levels in society. Members of the dominant culture, who assume that their middle-class norms are standard for all Americans, fail to realize that members of poverty groups do not always put the same value as they do on respect for law and order and on education, but they do value freedom of action. If members of minority cultures are to accept the kind of values that are essential to life in a highly technological society, they themselves must arrive at norms for which they can see the need. And this process must start in the groups closest to where the people live, in their neighborhoods.

EXPLICIT AND IMPLICIT NORMS

Explicit norms are those that are written down—laws, regulations, pledges, etc. Implicit norms are not stated, but they are just as effective in regulating behavior. Implicit norms may be at variance with the written norms of a group. For example, Christian churches generally adhere to the explicit norm "Love thy neighbor as thyself." Yet many lay and professional Christians actually operate, and require their fellows to operate, according to a norm that says in effect, "Love only those who are like you in education, race, socioeconomic level, breeding, etc."

In industry, as another example, production goals agreed to by labor leaders may differ markedly from the work norms of the workers themselves. In state agencies, goals set by authorities may vary from the written norms of local groups through which the agency works. In schools, the goal of developing mature students who can think for themselves often is contradicted by the norms of individual teachers who insist on a rote mastery of subject matter that discourages the ability to think.

Sometimes the explicit norms of the majority of a group are in conflict with the implicit norms of subgroups. The struggle over racial integration stems from this conflict. Sometimes neither the explicit nor the implicit norms contribute to the accomplishment of group goals.

If these conflicts are to be resolved at all, it will be only by the constant re-evaluation of both explicit and implicit norms and goals by the groups that seek to impose them.

COMMUNITY AND INDIVIDUAL NORMS AND GOALS

Individuals who are not members of any formal organization are affected little by community norms and goals. These nonmembers or fringe families will, of course, have goals and norms of their own, but these will generally be opposed to, or at least different from, those of the community and society at large. Community norms are effective only with those who are actually members of community organizations of one kind or another. Members of a subordinate culture can be persuaded to accept community norms only when they have been made functional members of such groups.

This gap between the norms of a community and those of its fringe members was demonstrated during the Korean War when a number of G.I.'s went over to the communists, much to the dismay of most Americans. When the Army made a study of these soldiers, it discovered that most came from city slums or from isolated rural areas. In either case, they were from fringe families that did not belong to organized groups of any kind outside their own extended families or peer groups. As a consequence they had never been effectively exposed to the American community norms that dictated the behavior of their fellow soldiers.

GROUP NORMS AND
INDIVIDUAL CHARACTER

As the sum total of his attitudes, values, and behavior patterns, an individual's character is largely shaped by the groups to which he is most loyal. Where there are conflicting loyalties, his character will be affected most by the group that satisfies his basic psychological needs. Since the family is best suited to satisfy these needs, its role is preeminent. When it does not perform this function, other groups sometimes with opposing norms and goals win the loyalty of the individual and influence his character formation for better or worse.

This does not mean that the family, or any other group, dictates permanently all the norms of its members. Far from it. It does, however, provide a framework for the individual's choice of norms so that when he moves into a totally different environment his attitudes and behavior can be predicted with reasonable accuracy.

REFERENCES AND READINGS

Batten, T. R. *Communities and their development.* London: Oxford University Press, 1957.

Goodenough, W. H. *Cooperation in change.* New York: Russell Sage Foundation, 1963.

Katz, E., & Lazarsfeld, P. F. *Personal influence.* New York: The Free Press, 1955.

Napier, R. W., & Gershenfeld, M. K. *Groups: Theory and experience.* Boston: Houghton Mifflin, 1973.

13
CONFORMITY PRESSURE

Conformity pressure is an attribute of all groups that can be used in a constructive manner to bring about change. Unfortunately the word "conformity" is emotionally loaded for many people. Some relate it to "groupism" and "togetherness" and see it as suppressing indivduality and standardizing behavior. For them conformity is largely responsible for destroying "the American ideal." Others hold that even greater conformity is needed if the social ideals we have long cherished are to be maintained against the assaults of rampant, uncontrolled individualism and libertinism.

What the extremists in both camps fail to recognize is that conformity is just one of the sociological facts of life. It bears the same relation to our sociological well-being that appetite does to our physical make-up: life would be pretty dull without appetite, yet misuse of it can lead to both psychological and physical discomfort.

CONFORMING INDIVIDUALISTS

In a society as complex as ours there are so many groups with conflicting norms that it is not always easy to distinguish the conformists from the individualists. Many people who appear to be individualists as they relate to one group are in actual fact conforming to the norms of other groups. In some cases they may be conforming to groups that exist only in their minds, groups whose ideal norms are set by great historical figures, such as Jesus and Mohammed or Jefferson and Lincoln. Other groups may have living leaders who have little direct relationship with most of their followers, yet their norms dominate the behavior of their followers and cause them to be seen as nonconformists by the community at large.

To the extent that members of a subordinate culture are isolated from formal community groups, they are thought of as individualists. In many cases, however, this isolation is due to circumstances over which these individuals have little control. When they are genuinely encouraged to participate in community organizations, and their psychological needs are fully satisfied in group activities, they usually show as much willingness to conform, whenever they are able to do so, as most people. When they fail to conform, the fault generally lies in the manner in which the group operates, not in the character of the individual.

PURPOSE OF CONFORMITY PRESSURE

Conformity pressure operates to make members adhere to a group's particular system of norms. The pressure itself is neutral from a value standpoint, neither good nor bad. But it can serve various ends and values—the ends of a Judeo-Christian democratic society on the one hand, or the ends of an atheistic, authoritarian, communist or fascist state on the other, for example.

Communist states have been adept at recognizing the power of conformity pressure and putting it to work. As they become highly industrialized, however, they face a dilemma. Success in a technological society requires the greatest possible freedom from the kind of restraints that party conformity demands. We can expect, therefore, that Russia and the communist states of Eastern Europe will increasingly relax their conformity pressure to the point where the party will no longer remain the unchallenged authority. In China and other underdeveloped communist countries, strict conformity to party discipline will have advantages for some time to come since the state of technology in these countries is still relatively low.

Historically, conformity pressure in the Christian church has been used for both good and bad purposes. In an earlier day, when society was far less complex, conformity pressure within the church helped maintain and transmit norms that were essential to civilized living, norms which are the foundations of our democratic society today. Occasionally, when maintenance of the institution of the church took priority over the needs of its members, conformity pressure was seriously misapplied.

CONDITIONS FOR SOUND USE
OF CONFORMITY PRESSURE

The question, then, is not whether conformity pressure is good or bad, but under what conditions it can be used to achieve the most desirable results in a democratic society.

First we must ask what the criteria are for the inclusion of members in a group—likenesses or differences. If the criteria include like-mindedness, a common background, and similar race, religion, education, economic class, and national origin, conformity pressure will operate to maintain likenesses and stability, but it will inhibit growth. On the other hand, if members are included *because* they are different and can make unique contributions to the group, conformity pressure will encourage healthy growth and change.

Even a cursory analysis of most community groups today will show that their membership is built around likenesses rather than differences. This is why so many of them find it difficult to move ahead in a mature fashion. Community action organizations, set up to deal with the problems of poverty, often make little headway despite enormous outlays of federal funds because of their total dependence on leadership drawn from either the dominant or the subordinate culture. If they can learn to involve members of both cultures, they may begin to progress.

The second question that needs to be asked is whether the standards of operation in the group include wide diffusion of leadership, respect for individual differences, recognition of each person's creative skills, and insistence upon free and open expression of opinion. If they do, the conformity pressure of the group will encourage originality, creativity, and independent judgment, while at the same time maximizing the satisfaction of the psychological needs of all group members. Thus, the norms arrived at by the group will get the strongest possible member support.

If, on the other hand, the standards of operation in the group demand uniform beliefs and attitudes, standardized behavior, the monopoly of leadership roles by a few, and suppression of criticism, independent thinking will be discouraged, creativity and originality inhibited, cooperative action limited, and the mature development of the group prevented. At the same time, the psychological needs of all but a few members will not be met and their desire to support group norms will be minimized.

PATTERN OF CONFORMITY PRESSURE

America was colonized by people who for the most part were trying to escape from restrictions in their religious and political life. For many years after the founding of the republic, her great appeal to the rest of the world lay in the fact that, relatively speaking, democratic standards of operation prevailed. By comparison with older nations, America respected individual differences in the immigrants that came to her shores. Her people recognized and used the creative skills the immigrants brought with them and tolerated, if not always encouraged, the free and open expression of opinion about government, values, and ways of life. As a result, America became one of the most dynamic societies in all history, strong and affluent and with a high degree of adaptability to a changing world.

As a society grows older and less mobile, however, its institutions tend to become more and more restrictive. As a consequence, some isolated communities have developed such restrictive standards of group operation that very little semblance of democracy remains. These communities have, in a sense, strangled themselves. High unemployment rates, low educational levels, and low average living standards prevail, and a wide gap exists between the dominant and the subordinate classes. Fortunately, communities in which mobility is high, have, in varying degrees, escaped this sad fate.

Due to the impact of outside programs, some communities have broken away from their restrictive pattern and are beginning to operate according to more democratic standards. The resulting release of human resources is bringing social, economic, and spiritual benefits to all concerned.

STRENGTH OF CONFORMITY PRESSURE

Members of a group will seek conformity as they see that it is necessary in order to accomplish group goals or individual goals through the group. Where group goals are vague or not an essential part of group life, conformity pressure will be relaxed, and only those norms that are necessary to sustain the group will be maintained.

The strength of conformity pressure is determined by four factors: (1) the amount of attraction the group holds for its members; (2) the importance to the group of the issue on which conformity is demanded; (3) the awareness that the group's norms are unanimously supported by others; and (4) the size of the group supporting the norms.

These factors are not fixed in their relative importance. In fact, size and group attraction may offset each other in some respects. The larger the group, the less likely it is to fully satisfy the deep psychological needs of its members. Yet the more adherents there are to group norms, the greater will be the group pressure to support them.

GROUP MEMBERS' MOTIVATION

If a group is to move toward the accomplishment of its goals, group members must perform a number of functions. The more these harmonize and integrate into an overall pattern, the more successfully the group will achieve its goal. How well this is done depends on:

1. how much individuals are attracted to membership in the group;
2. the prestige of the group in the eyes of its members;
3. the extent to which members like each other;
4. the extent to which members share in the choice of a goal to be accomplished;
5. the extent to which they see the fulfillment of individual goals in the group goal; and
6. the importance group members place on the individual functions they are to perform in accomplishing the group goal.

It would be impossible to say which of these factors are most important. Each member of the group will be affected differently. A person with many friends in all the groups he belongs to may not be affected by his relations with the members of any one group and be more concerned with the prestige of a group. Or he may see a group goal as a means of accomplishing important personal goals. Another person, who has limited social contacts, may be motivated primarily by his friendly relations with the members of a specific group.

If interpersonal factors largely determine group members' motivation, the group leader should focus his attention on procedures rather than on goals as such. The more he concentrates his efforts on the group's method of operation and on the creation of a climate in which everyone feels free to express his real feelings, the more he will stimulate group movement or locomotion.

When group locomotion is proceeding well, members will be more concerned with getting the job done than with who performs a particular function; they will be more attracted to each other as they cooperate toward group and personal goals; and they will more readily accept suggestions from other members since they will recognize that they are all helping each other.

The stimulation of group motivation is an essential function of group-oriented leadership. If either an appointed leader or individual members allow themselves to be guided by personal needs that are not consonant with a group's goals, locomotion will be hampered. When the leader is determined to "have his way" or is convinced that he knows better than the rest how to identify needs, determine solutions, and achieve goals, he is placing the satisfaction of his personal needs above the attainment of group goals and hindering group locomotion.

What is most important in a group's total life picture is not its final accomplishment but its pursuit of its own goals even when these are seen by outsiders as mistaken ones. In the final analysis, group maturity is the paramount concern—and this includes the right to make mistakes.

REFERENCES AND READINGS

Cartwright, D., & Zander, A. *Group dynamics: Research and theory* (3rd ed.). New York: Harper & Row, 1968.

Cartwright, D., & Lippitt, R. Group dynamics and the individual. In W. K. Bennis, K. D. Benne, & R. Chin (Eds.), *The planning of change*. New York: Holt, Rinehart & Winston, 1962.

Dentler, R. A., & Erikson, K. T. The functions of deviance in groups. In T. M. Mills & S. Rosenberg (Eds.), *Readings on the sociology of small groups*. Englewood Cliffs, N.J.: Prentice Hall, 1970.

14
THE PRINCIPLES OF GROUP PROCESS

Members of many community development organizations think of change in the abstract and fail to relate it to people. They talk about the school dropout problem, the lack of employment opportunities, or the need for community beautification as if these things could be dealt with apart from the men and women, boys and girls, whose attitudes, values, and behavior have a direct bearing on the solution of the problem.

Without exception, solving community problems requires the changing of someone's values, attitudes, or behavior in some way. If nothing more, people have to overcome their indifference to the conditions that constitute the problem. Many communities discover that there is an astounding public apathy about the number of young people who enter adulthood unprepared to hold down the simplest of jobs, about the number of families who live in conditions of extreme poverty, or about the way our surroundings are made unlivable from day to day through carelessness and selfishness. When the human factor in these problems is overlooked, they never get solved because the norms that cause them remain unchanged.

It is not enough, therefore, for boards of community organizations to agree what community needs are and develop programs to meet them. The people who are in any way related to the problem or its solution—for instance, the parents of school dropouts, the dropouts themselves, the teachers, and the school administrators—are the ones whose norms will have to be changed before a real solution can be found to the dropout problem. This cannot be accomplished without their being involved personally in the process. Many of them can be reached only at the neighborhood level, hence the desirability of creating neighborhood organizations in as many localities as possible. In these organizations, problems can be identified and solutions agreed upon. An overall community program is then built on a consolidation of the needs of all the neighborhood groups.

If these neighborhood organizations operate according to certain well-established principles, the pressure for conformity within them will help to bring about those changes in people's norms that are necessary to the solution of the problems. A number of these principles are particularly valuable and should be used as guidelines in the operation of voluntary organizations of all kinds (Cartwright, 1951).[1]

THE PRINCIPLE OF FELT NEEDS

The more group members discover for themselves the need for change, the stronger will be the pressure for change from within the group.

This does not mean that professionals working with the organization are helpless to bring about change. They can accomplish a great deal when they have learned to work beforehand with and through individual group leaders and then keep themselves in the background during community meetings. They should have faith that these leaders will know the needs of the community better than they do and how far the community's resources will go in achieving solutions.

THE PRINCIPLE OF INDIGENOUS LEADERSHIP

Change can be brought about most effectively when the persons working for change are considered without reservation to be members in full of the group.

Even professional workers who have lived for years in a community are not really members in full of the groups with which they work. The fact that ministers, county agents, home agents, social workers, community action directors, and many other agency employees are being paid to work with the people sets them apart from the other members of the group.

THE PRINCIPLE OF GROUP ATTRACTION

The more attractive a group is to its members the greater the influence it can exert on them.

This principle considers the question of what constitutes the basis of an individual's attraction to a group. In middle-class society, due to training that begins early in childhood, people generally join groups because of their *interests*. Their membership in a group continues as long as the group satisfies their psychological needs. Among the hard-

---

[1]Dorwin Cartwright, "Achieving Change in People" in HUMAN RELATIONS, New York, Plenum Corp., Vol. IV, No. 4, 1951, pp. 381-392. The wording of the three principles is used here by permission of the publishers.

core poor, however, relationships have usually developed around the satisfaction of psychological needs within the family and in peer groups. Because children in such families are rarely exposed to groups devoted to specific interests, as they grow up they are seldom attracted by organizations that put interests foremost—even when these groups are organized primarily to benefit them.

ATTRACTION BY INTEREST

Interests are of four different kinds.

1. *Groups can help to achieve goals that the individual cannot as easily achieve on his own.* People join various kinds of groups to improve their physical, mental, or spiritual well-being or to achieve social, political, or economic ends through cooperative action. Since many groups exist in almost every community to satisfy these personal needs, the holding power of any one group is slight when based on interest alone. When one group proves unsatisfactory for any reason, a person can readily switch to another and still achieve his goal.

2. *The activities of the group are attractive to the members.* Individuals join both formal and informal groups to play bridge, bowl, swim, dance, or study the stock market; to discuss international affairs, art, literature, music, gardening, or a host of other topics. Since it is the activity that is important, people can easily transfer their membership to more "congenial" groups when their relationships with one group "sour." Or they can drop the activity altogether for reasons of health, aging, or increasing responsibilities elsewhere. In any case the groups themselves are relatively unimportant in the lives of most people.

3. *Membership in the group is a path to goals outside the group.* People often join professional or political organizations because these give them access to individuals on whom their advancement or their business interests depend, or because the group provides them with the right label for the conduct of their professional activities. In some states, for example, success in legal practice may depend largely on belonging to the right political party.

Circumstances may change so that association with any one group is no longer desirable or necessary. If status was the original goal, the individual may then begin to look around for more prestigious groups to join.

4. *Group membership may be a means of providing security against a real or imagined danger.* The rapid changes taking place in our society today frighten many people into joining groups for protection against forces and individuals that threaten their chosen way of life. As long as these people can be convinced that the danger exists, they will retain membership in such groups.

ATTRACTION BY PSYCHOLOGICAL NEEDS

Most groups, regardless of the interests they are focused on, satisfy deep psychological needs of their members and, in some cases, these needs may be the chief force that holds the group together. In fact, some groups continue to exist long after the interest factors that brought them together have ceased to function because the groups have come to serve the psychological needs of their members so well.

The psychological needs that the individual can satisfy only in his interpersonal relationships—that is, in groups—can be classified in four categories.

1. *The need for response* (fellowship) is usually satisfied in the kind of group activities in which people rub shoulders and forget their status differences. The formal type of organization program, which may be concentrated on the "interest" that brought the members of the group together, usually leaves little time for this type of activity.

The shy member of the woman's club who finds herself chatting easily about family problems with "Mrs. Gottrocks" while washing dishes after the club's refreshment hour may acquire a sense of fellowship which she has never known before. Likewise the laborer who has never felt at ease in community club meetings may find a very real sense of fellowship during the building of the community center when working alongside the banker, the school superintendent, and the business man. Wealth and community status are forgotten as they swap stories while they lay cinder block. The laborer is appreciated as a person, and this in turn helps him to satisfy his need for response in a way it has not been satisfied before.

In organizations that meet regularly, recreational activities can help provide this sense of fellowship, especially if they are varied and the emphasis is on having a good time rather than on competition or entertainment. What kind of recreation this should be differs from group to group.

2. *The need for security*, that is, the sense of belonging, or the "we" feeling, is satisfied when all members are involved in making major decisions and when each member feels that his opinion is as important as that of others in group deliberations.

Important issues should be discussed by the membership as a whole, rather than being shunted off to a committee for discussion and decision. And if the group is too large for everyone to participate freely, it should be broken up into buzz groups. Even when members do not at first agree with the final decision, they will recognize it as a group decision in which they had a part, and they will support it.

Some organizations are bound by their constitutions to abide by the decisions of boards of directors, boards of deacons, and the like. In such cases the members may become increasingly alienated from the organization because they feel no real part in it and lack the sense of security they need. The constitutions of most such organizations do not rule out the discussion of issues by the membership as a whole and the expression of the wishes of the members on these issues. A board that is genuinely interested in strengthening the organization should welcome member opinions on vital issues and recognize its own role as the ratification of such wishes once they have been expressed by the group.

3. *The need for recognition (self-expression)* is satisfied when individual capabilities are recognized and used to further the group's goals.

Too many groups fail to satisfy this need. There can be a monopoly of leadership roles by a few—which usually means that recognition is restricted to those who probably need it least. A handful of status leaders may get credit for accomplishments that others have made important contributions to. And the group's activities can be so limited in scope that many people with a wide variety of usable capabilities are overlooked.

When an organization's program includes a wide range of activities, people with diverse skills can participate and gain recognition for their contributions. Adding a social and recreation hour to a community program can provide such opportunities and also greatly improve group fellowship.

4. *The need to do the "forbidden"* occurs when the needs for response, security, and recognition are not satisfied, and individuals turn to "thrills": exceeding a speed law, committing vandalism, or participating in violence and destruction. When young people are involved in delinquency cases, it can almost always be demonstrated that their families or peer groups failed to satisfy one or more of their psychological needs and, as a consequence, they seek to satisfy this fourth need. In the same way, people in slum areas, minority racial groups, or students in large universities seek various forms of "kicks" in retaliation for society's failure to satisfy their other psychological needs.

The answer to this need lies in satisfying the other three basic psychological needs—if not by individual families, then by neighborhood organizations and other groups within the community.

The three psychological needs can be satisfied in voluntary organizations in the following manner.

- *Response:* Name tags should be used to make sure that all members are known by name to one another. All members should be involved in activities such as recreation, community singing, social hours, and suppers where they have an opportunity to discover what they have in common with fellow members, not what sets them apart.

- *Security:* All important decisions should be made by all concerned members of the group. This is a slow process but it is necessary if there is to be full member support of group decisions. Small groups should be used whenever possible in making decisions.

- *Recognition:* Desirable functions for which there is recognition should be shared by all members, not monopolized by a few leaders. Broadening the organization's program to allow new skills to be brought into play is also helpful.

THE RELATION OF INTERESTS TO PSYCHOLOGICAL NEEDS

What has been said about interests and psychological needs is true in varying degrees of all groups in both the dominant and the subordinate cultures of our society. A point that needs to be stressed, however, is that people in the subordinate cultures will be influenced much less by the interest factors and much more by the manner in which groups satisfy their psychological needs. Members from subordinate cultures who participate little in group activities and seldom assume responsibility will remain fringe members if their psychological needs are not satisfied within the group. If they cannot forget the differences (in speech, clothes, or manners, for example) that set them off from the others, if their opinions are seldom sought, and if no attempt is made to utilize their skills, their tenuous attraction to the group and lack of support for its goals will not change. At their first contact with a group, therefore, every effort should be made to make them feel at home, to make them feel that their ideas or reactions deserve consideration by the group, and to give them a sense of significance in the group.

REFERENCES AND READINGS

Bennis, W. G., & Shepard, H. A. A theory of group development. In T. M. Mills & S. Rosenberg (Eds.), *Readings on the sociology of small groups*. Englewood Cliffs, N.J.: Prentice Hall, 1970.

Bradford, L. P. Group forces affecting learning. In C. G. Kemp (Ed.), *Perspectives on the group process*. Boston: Houghton Mifflin, 1970.

Cartwright, D. Achieving change in people. In W. G. Bennis, K. D. Benne, & R. Chin (Eds.), *The planning of change*. New York: Holt, Rinehart & Winston, 1962.

McGregor, D. *The human side of enterprise*. New York: McGraw-Hill, 1960.

15

THE CIRCULAR PROCESS OF SOCIAL INTERACTION

The success of a group in carrying out its task depends a great deal on the personal relations between members. Often these relationships take on a fixed pattern early in the life of a group, blocking a whole store of resources that would greatly facilitate accomplishment of the group's objectives.

In such a situation the contribution each member is able to make is determined not so much by his capabilities as by the notions other people acquire about him at the start. What he does subsequently fortifies their misconceptions and his attempts to change his status and his effectiveness in the group are to no avail.

The concept of the circular process of social interaction throws considerable light on the relationships among group members and explains why this "vicious circle" effect takes place. It also suggests how this can be changed. The process can be divided into four steps (See Figure 15.1).

1. *The Process Within a Member*. Every member enters a group with fairly well-defined feelings abut himself. He wants to be liked, respected, and considered important. Or he fears he will be disliked, scorned, and considered insignificant. Of course, there are various gradations between these two extremes.

These feelings about himself affect his attitude toward others. For example, if he thinks too highly of himself, he is less likely to think well of others. However, what he thinks about them may also be created by what he has heard beforehand or what he expects from the group situation itself. Such inner processes shape an individual's intentions toward others.

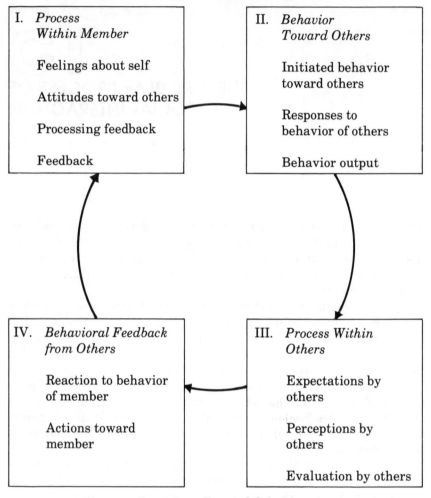

Intentions Toward Member

I. *Process* *Within Member* Feelings about self Attitudes toward others Processing feedback Feedback	II. *Behavior* *Toward Others* Initiated behavior toward others Responses to behavior of others Behavior output
IV. *Behavioral Feedback* *from Others* Reaction to behavior of member Actions toward member	III. *Process Within* *Others* Expectations by others Perceptions by others Evaluation by others

Intentions Toward Others

Figure 15.1.   The Circular Process

2. *Behavior Toward Others*. The member may initiate behavior, or may react to behavior from others. In his desire to "get started on the right foot," he may walk up to the other members of the group, offer his hand in friendly greeting, and introduce himself. The response he gets will play an important part in his later reaction to the group. Or he may be the recipient of similar friendly advances and think of them

as forms of condescension, "apple polishing," or "politicking." On the other hand, he may treat them at face value. In any case what he does under the circumstances may be called his *behavior output* to which the other members of the group react.

3. *Process Within Others.* The others in the group have attitudes and feelings about themselves and their fellow members which inevitably affect their reaction to an individual member. They bring to the group certain expectations about him. These may be personal, based upon something they have heard about him, or they may be stereotypes relating to his job, socioeconomic status, religious affiliation, race, or the nationality of his family. In any case these expectations color their perception of his behavior and determine their evaluation of his behavior output.

This evaluation shapes their intentions toward the member. If they see him as "throwing his weight around" because of his self-assurance or "with a chip on his shoulder" because he is shy and speaks only under pressure, they may try to "put him in his place."

4. *Behavioral Feedback from Others.* This includes action toward the member that may take place even before he has had a chance to express himself, or there may be reactions to him following some remark or gesture he has made. Because of his own perception of himself, in relation to the situation he is in, this feedback may be seriously distorted. He may take as a personal affront what is in reality only a careless mannerism of his fellows. From here on he is involved in processing feedback to determine his future behavior and his attitudes to the other members of the group.

And so the process goes on and on, often creating a "group personality" that is far removed from an individual's real self and that differs markedly from the personality he exhibits in other groups in which a friendlier atmosphere allows him to be more fully himself.

A HYPOTHETICAL CASE

To better understand the circular process of social interaction, let us take a hypothetical individual through the four steps (See Figure 15.2).

1. *Process Within Member.* Our group member is a really capable individual who, however, is not at his best in group situations. He tends to be shy and retiring in the presence of others except for his close friends and so will hold back his resources from the group.

Since he is genuinely capable and knows many of the answers that the group is struggling to obtain, his inability to enter into the discussion leads to internal pressure to express or conceal feelings. The more this pressure builds, the less normal will be his mode of expression

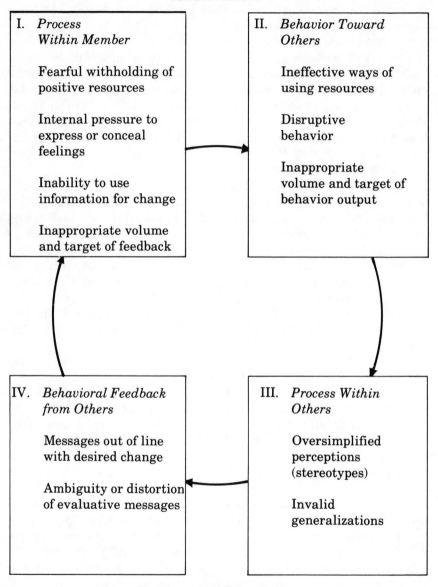

Inappropriate Intentions
Toward Others

I. *Process
Within Member*

Fearful withholding of
positive resources

Internal pressure to
express or conceal
feelings

Inability to use
information for change

Inappropriate volume
and target of feedback

II. *Behavior Toward
Others*

Ineffective ways of
using resources

Disruptive
behavior

Inappropriate
volume and target of
behavior output

IV. *Behavioral Feedback
from Others*

Messages out of line
with desired change

Ambiguity or distortion
of evaluative messages

III. *Process Within
Others*

Oversimplified
perceptions
(stereotypes)

Invalid
generalizations

Inappropriate Intentions
Toward Member

Figure 15.2.   A Hypothetical Case

when he does speak up. The pitch and volume of his voice may rise to an unpleasant level, his tone may seem an angry one, and his whole manner may appear offensive. Even while he is talking he will sense that what he is saying is being rejected, and this leads him to inappropriate intentions toward others.

2. *Behavior Toward Others*. It is now even harder for the member to make a satisfactory contribution to the group. If the pressures are strong enough he may indulge in disruptive behavior and express his resentment of the treatment he is receiving from others by making cutting remarks or by disparaging their contributions. He attacks personalities rather than problems and makes a major issue out of what is of minor importance to the group. He is now under pressure to assert himself.

3. *Process Within Others*. The others in the group seldom take the time, even if they could, to analyze the situation. The group member's behavior leads them to oversimplified perceptions or stereotypes about him. They now see him as a "blow-hard" or someone with "a chip on his shoulder." These invalid generalizations about him result in inappropriate intentions such as wanting to "squelch him" or "put him in his place."

4. *Behavioral Feedback from Others*. When the others have stereotyped the member's behavior, they may respond to him in an ambiguous or distorted form. In fact, the communication between him and the others has little or no bearing on the task at hand. Messages are out of line with the desired change.

Consequently, as the member sees it, the feedback he has received from the others tells him little about the contributions he tried to make to the group's discussion, but it seems to tell him a lot about his status in the group and the other members' reaction to his personality.

The two "normal" responses that he can make to this type of feedback are insensitivity or defense. If he is thickskinned or has become hardened by similar experiences in the past, he will remain insensitive to the attitudes and behavior of the others in the group. He will accept their reaction as normal and thereby fulfill the stereotype of himself as having "a chip on his shoulder." He may even be disappointed if they do not react this way, since he has learned to expect such treatment and finds in it assurance that at least he is getting recognition. On the other hand, he could try to build up defenses for himself, finding ulterior reasons for his being rejected. Often he will see himself as an "outsider"—he is a well-rounded intellectual, the group members are unenlightened technicians.

In either case, the final result as far as the group member is concerned will be his inability to use information for change. Since he does not know that it was his voice or his manner of speaking that was at fault, not his contribution or his personality, there is little that he can do to change the situation. Neither he nor the other members of the group have benefited from his presence and any future contributions he might make to the group are lost.

THE LOOKING GLASS SELF

Two questions that naturally come to mind in regard to this circular process of social interaction are (1) How does it get started the way it does? and (2) How can we change it? As we have seen, some of the most important factors in the process are the attitudes that the group member holds about himself at the start. Often these feelings about self bear little or no relation to his real capabilities.

The best and most easily understood explanation of how this happens can be found in a concept called "The Looking Glass Self," developed by Charles Horton Cooley (1922). According to this concept every individual in his earliest childhood develops a picture of his own personality as he sees himself in the eyes of his parents and of others in his immediate environment. If his parents, for example, look upon the child with loving approval, praising him for whatever he does and perhaps excusing his mistakes, the child is apt to grow up with a high degree of self-confidence.

On the other hand, if the parents demand that he measure up to the accomplishments of an older brother or sister or some ideal that exists only in their minds and constantly frown upon his inability to reach this standard, his self-confidence will be greatly shaken. He may early develop what used to be known as an inferiority complex.

In either case, his image of himself bears little relation either to his potential or to his known capabilities. The shy child whose parents are disappointed because he is not an outstanding scholar may have real potential for becoming an artist or an athlete. The completely confident child may reveal little ability in any field, but the chances are good that he will "get by" in life on his personality. He will "charm" other people into doing the job for which he may get the credit.

If there are others besides the parents in whose eyes the child can see himself in his everyday activities, he stands a better chance of developing a more realistic concept of himself. His brothers and sisters near the same age, for example, may encourage him in activities that their parents frown on but that build his self-confidence because these activities are in line with his capabilities.

An individual who remains in much the same surroundings all his life often retains this childhood image of his personality until he dies.

When an individual has to adjust to a completely different social environment, however, and has to gain acceptance from people that have very different value systems from his own, his personality may undergo a change.

A group or organization that recognizes that to reach its goals it needs to fully utilize the resources of all its members can do a great deal to overcome personality handicaps that limit its members' contributions. Before tackling its assigned task, the group should undertake a series of sessions for constructive criticism of members' behavior. Each member can take a turn acting as group facilitator for the discussion of different topics, preferably ones that are not emotionally loaded. When several have tried their hand at being facilitators, the group can offer constructive criticism of how well each member played the facilitator role and how the performance of the group as a whole was or was not enhanced by this mode of operation. Then the group can move on to practice the functional roles of leadership. As these functions are mastered, and the nonfunctional roles eliminated, the members will build greater confidence in their performance as a group and they will seek help from each other in overcoming their individual handicaps. They will become a more mature group in which all make their maximum contribution.

REFERENCES AND READINGS

Cooley, C. H. *Human nature and the social order*. New York: Charles Scribner's, 1922.

Culbert, S. A. The interpersonal process of self-disclosure: It takes two to see one. In R. Hacon (Ed.), *Personal and organizational effectiveness*. Maidenhead, England: McGraw-Hill, 1972.

Giffin, K., & Patton, B. R. *Fundamentals of interpersonal communication*. New York: Harper & Row, 1971.

Harris, T. A. *I'm OK-you're OK*. New York: Harper & Row, 1969.

16

THE ROLE OF LEADERSHIP IN GROUP ACTIVITY

How well a group can strengthen its attraction for members will generally depend on the caliber and understanding of its leaders. Many who try to be good leaders fail because they have misconceptions about their roles. Two modern concepts of leadership may help clarify what is expected of a leader and how leaders can be developed. The two are complementary, rather than contradictory, and apply to different group situations.

THE SITUATIONAL CONCEPT OF LEADERSHIP

Many communities and organizations, which are said to be "dead" because they do not have effective leaders, have a great deal of untapped leadership potential. Their problem is apt to be one of two mentioned previously: leadership roles are monopolized by status leaders who do not have the knowledge or skills needed to help fulfill group purposes; or the organization's activities are so restricted that individuals with a wealth of knowledge and skills sit idly by. In either case, a few uninspired individuals can assume leadership in a limited variety of activities in which they happen to have some competence.

While organizations in the dominant culture are not exempt, these limitations are much more prevalent in subcultures and are often the reason why people in low-income neighborhoods lack faith in the effectiveness of organizational activity of any kind.

Status leaders are rarely motivated to correct such situations. Instead they, and others who monopolize the few existing leadership roles, are jealous of their positions of influence and oppose the development of new leaders who might challenge that influence. Thus, "dead" communities and organizations are rarely changed from within.

More often, professional workers coming from outside introduce programs in which local people can use their specific skills to help achieve new goals relevant to the group's needs. In this way they begin the process of leadership development. These outside professional workers may represent federal or state agencies, community action organizations covering county or multicounty areas, denominational headquarters, or regional planning district commissions. They encourage local people to organize and analyze their needs, help identify local people who have the knowledge and skills essential to effecting change, and see that these latter are given an opportunity to use their skills to help achieve group goals. In this way they begin the process of leadership development.

Qualities of a Leader

According to the situational concept, *a leader is a person, recognized as having the know-how needed by the organization, who is put into a situation where he can use that know-how to help the group.*

What the know-how is depends on the needs of the group at any stage in its activities. It may be the ability to lead a discussion or preside at a meeting, to involve group members in recreational activities, to carry out a specific farm, home, or community improvement such as building a trench silo, freezing garden vegetables, or laying cement block for a community center. The opportunities for leadership development are limited only by the varieties of know-how required. In every group there will almost always be individuals whose superior know-how in any activity motivates other members to acquire the skills they need to help the group achieve its goals.

It is not enough for the potential leader simply to have know-how, however. His fellows must recognize that he has it. A college-educated young farmer with all the latest agricultural techniques at his fingertips, whose neighbors look askance at his newfangled and, to them, costly practices, is not good leadership material until the neighbors agree that his ideas are sound. On the other hand, even with out-of-date information a person can still be an effective leader if his neighbors credit him with having the necessary know-how and if those who create the leadership situation help him bring his ideas in line with modern practices. In any event, the potential leader needs to be put in a situation where he can use his know-how to help the group accomplish its goals.

Types of Emerging Leaders

While leadership springs from group situations, situations do not dictate what kind of leader will emerge. If no capable local individuals are available, the group may have recourse to a *static leader*, an outside expert who knows the answers but develops no bonds between himself and the group members he is working with. Often such an agency specialist only supplies technical information or procedures. In some cases his responsibilities to the group, and the frequency of his visits to it, may create personal bonds and he may move from a static to a dynamic relationship with members. In this case, however, he runs the danger of preventing, instead of encouraging, the development of local leadership. He needs to impart his information through chosen members of the group, strengthen their leadership capabilities, and so forestall the group's becoming dependent on him.

Dynamic leaders are of several kinds, depending on the type of bond that exists between them and their following.

1. The *adhesive or institutional* leader is a functionary of an institution such as a church, school, or government. People assume that because he is recognized as a leader within his own institution he ought to be able to tackle any leadership job. Ministers, school officials, agency representatives, and political office holders are often called upon to accept community leadership roles for this reason. While they may be capable, they may not always have as much know-how as some untried leaders. Furthermore, adhesive leaders may be so surfeited with recognition and responsibilities that they are not motivated to do as much for the group as others might do.

2. The *impressive* leader wants to gain power or influence over others. He will recognize a common cause with the group only so long as it serves his own ends to do so. Often such an individual helps the group achieve very considerable goals only to lose interest when a more prestigious organization offers him leadership with a broader scope, or when he is invited to move up to a regional or state level within the same organization. Seeking influential positions is human enough and is not necessarily a trait limited to an impressive leader. The drawback is that this ego-centered individual fails to encourage the development of other leaders within the group, so that when he moves on, there is no one prepared to fill his place.

3. Finally, there is the *expressive* leader who achieves power and recognizes that his own interests are best served with and through the group. Under his guidance, leadership responsibilities are shared by all members of the group so that at any time the group can carry on without his being present.

In setting up organizational activities of any kind, we cannot ignore the *adhesive* or *impressive* types of leaders any more than we can ignore *status* leaders. Among all three types are many who have monopolized leadership roles in the past and are jealous of the power and prestige their activities have given them. If they are asked to assume community leadership, they may subordinate the community program to their institutional or personal ends, or they may lack the motivation to take positive action for the community because they are inclined to be satisfied with things as they are.

If emphasis is put on securing the individual who has more know-how than anyone else, there is a chance that these other types of leaders may even help find the right person. They may not equate know-how with leadership and hence have no cause to feel threatened.

Identifying Potential Leaders of the Expressive Type

People capable of expressive leadership are not always easy to identify because they are not likely to seek leadership. They may not even think of themselves as leaders, and others may not consider them so, either. They stand out only in that other members of the group want to talk with them before making up their minds and others instinctively imitate them in certain areas of activity.

We cannot locate them by asking, "Who are your leaders?" because, more often than not, the responses will lead to *adhesive* or *impressive* types of dynamic leaders or to *status* leaders. Instead, we find these potential leaders by asking questions related to the group's activities, such as "Who would you turn to for help in organizing a recreation program for young people?" "Which person knows best how to teach underprivileged children to read and write?" "Which person in the neighborhood could most effectively get neighbors together for home management instruction?"

The people located in this way may have nothing but know-how. They may have no stage presence, no ability to talk to people in groups, no poise, and no organizing ability. But these things can be changed. And if their know-how is out of date, this, too, can be corrected. The important thing is that they are recognized as having it.

THE FUNCTIONAL CONCEPT OF LEADERSHIP

In the past a great deal that has been written about leadership has left the impression that a leader is a very special kind of individual on whom the group depends for its existence and that he is usually born to fill a role for which only a few are qualified. We now know, however, that every member of a group can be trained to fill a leadership role. In a mature group, each person at one time or another functions as a leader and as a follower.

Seen in this light, leadership is the performance of a wide variety of specific functions needed to accomplish a task. It strengthens the relations of individual members to the group. Individuals differ markedly in the number and kind of functions they can perform, although skill in performing many of the functions can be acquired. The more these functions are shared by all group members, the more mature the group can be said to be.

The functions or roles fall into two categories: *task roles* and *group maintenance roles*.

Task Roles

1. *Initiating activity:* suggesting new ideas, new approaches, new ways of organizing material, or offering solutions.
2. *Seeking information:* asking others to supply needed information or clarification of data on hand.
3. *Seeking opinions:* getting others to evaluate ideas or procedures already suggested.
4. *Giving information:* providing the group with facts or experience relevant to the question at hand.
5. *Giving opinions:* expressing a belief about the value of ideas or procedures under consideration.
6. *Elaborating:* building onto an idea already suggested so that it will better meet the needs of the group.
7. *Coordinating:* relating various ideas before the group so that they become a connected whole.
8. *Summarizing:* restating briefly the important contributions made to the group so that none will be overlooked, and bringing the group together in its thinking.
9. *Testing feasibility:* applying the ideas to real-life situations in order to pretest their effect and to anticipate and avoid mistakes.
10. *Testing for consensus:* asking for group opinions in a tentative manner to determine if the group is ready to make a decision.

How many of the task roles will need to be fulfilled in any given situation will depend on the complexity of the task at hand. In any case, the more these roles are performed by different group members rather than by the designated leader, the more effective the group will be. Yet if only the task roles are played, the group may arrive at a decision but lack the motivating force to implement it, and members will have little desire to continue working with the group. Maintenance functions need to be performed if members are to support group norms and goals and remain eager to be involved.

Group-Maintenance Roles

1. *Encouraging:* being sincerely warm and friendly to others and encouraging them to participate by being positive about their contributions. This includes thoughtful consideration of both the merits and weaknesses of contributions made by the less-outspoken members of the group.

2. *Gatekeeping:* making it possible for individuals to be brought into the discussion by asking for their ideas or opinions and, in some cases, by restraining more vocal members so that others have a chance to talk.

3. *Standard setting:* expressing standards or criteria for group operation which will help the group arrive at decisions objectively and amicably.

4. *Expressing group feelings:* summarizing how the group seems to feel about an issue.

5. *Diagnosing:* determining sources of difficulty and proposing the appropriate next steps.

6. *Compromising:* trying to provide compromises for opposing points of view, raising questions whose answers will eliminate misunderstanding, or offering to modify one's own position in order to achieve group agreement.

7. *Harmonizing:* draining off negative feelings with humor or shifting to a broader point of view.

8. *Consensus testing:* sending up a trial balloon to test a possible group conclusion.

9. *Following:* serving as an interested listener while others are talking.

Group maintenance roles are far less effective when performed only, or primarily, by the designated leader rather than by other group members. In fact, some roles such as that of *encourager* may bring out negative reactions when performed by the leader. A shy group member, for example, may feel he is "being put on the spot" and may "freeze" when asked for his opinion by the chairman, yet respond willingly enough when asked by another member of the group.

Anyone who has sat through a group discussion where each person was interested only in his own ideas will appreciate how important the role of follower is. It does no good for a person to try to make a contribution to the group if no one else pays attention to him. Granted, some people may be listening when they seem to be doing something else, but for a group to be truly effective all members have to learn to communicate their interest in what other members have to say. Without this a group can make no genuine progress as a group. For this reason following can be considered to be a leadership function that is essential to group maintenance.

Nonfunctional Roles

Group members in immature groups will sometimes seek to satisfy individual needs that are irrelevant to the group task and harmful to the group. The roles they play in this way may be called nonfunctional roles.

1. *Being aggresive:* trying to deflate the status of others, disapproving of their contributions, or joking aggressively about them.
2. *Blocking:* opposing unreasonably, being stubbornly resistant.
3. *Recognition seeking:* calling attention to oneself by boasting, name dropping, or mentioning personal achievements.
4. *Self-confessing:* expressing personal feelings that have no bearing on the group or its task.
5. *Being a playboy:* making a conscious display of noninvolvement in the group's activity by whispering, writing notes, engaging in horseplay, or reading something not relevant to the task at hand.
6. *Dominating:* asserting authority or superiority over the group by giving directions, interrupting others, or flattering members.
7. *Help seeking:* taking advantage of the group meeting to try to solve a personal problem or gain sympathy.
8. *Special-interest pleading:* cloaking one's own prejudices by claiming to speak for "the housewife," "the small farmer," or "the general public."

Through practice, group members can learn to distinguish the functional from the nonfunctional roles and, in time, eliminate the latter.

THE ROLE OF THE
DESIGNATED LEADER

If a group is to become mature, develop to the full its task and group maintenance roles, and minimize its nonfunctional roles, it has to have guidance at the start. This guidance should be provided by the designated leader or chairman. Such a person should try to become just another member of the group, indistinguishable from the other members, but until this is accomplished he will need to assume certain responsibilities.

1. He should establish a permissive social climate in which every group member will feel free to participate; see that the physical setting is comfortable and put everyone on an equal basis; make sure that everyone is personally acquainted with all other group members and can call them by name.

2. He should help the group organize itself and determine the procedures it will follow.

3. He should facilitate communication by occasionally playing those roles that are needed but not yet assumed by other group members, but he should avoid doing this so often that the group depends on him for it.

4. He should help the group learn from experience by encouraging the evaluation of their efforts and showing where important functions have not been performed.

5. He should make himself dispensable as soon as possible.

DEVELOPING A MATURE GROUP

In order to mature, the group needs to know what the different functional and nonfunctional roles are and which of them they habitually play or fail to play as they operate. They can do this by using Group Leadership Role Check Sheets, such as those given in Appendix II, letting each member check the roles he believes he and the others played during the session. These can be tallied to show how much agreement there is between the roles individuals think they have played and the roles they think others in the group have played. Where there is serious disagreement, clarification of the roles is in order. The group can also appoint persons to observe the roles while a group discussion is going on; then their observations can be tallied with the group's analysis. In these two ways group members can uncover nonfunctional roles that are also a detriment to the group's well-being. They can also learn to recognize task and group-maintenance roles that they ought to be playing to improve the group's performance.

This criticism of member roles is most effective when done impersonally at first. When the majority agrees that someone has played a blocking, dominating, or recognition-seeking role, for example, it is not necessary to name names. As a rule, the offending person will be aware of his behavior and will be motivated to avoid it in the future. On the other hand, credit can be given to individuals who have played needed functional roles, and occasionally suggestions can be made to the group as to how these roles could have been even more effective.

As members become accustomed to this type of group procedure, they will begin asking such questions as "Was I dominating?" "Why wasn't Joe brought into the discussion; wasn't anybody interested in his opinion?" or "Would it have helped if someone had summarized the points already made before we tried to move on?"

Self-evaluation can also help members become aware of their performance as a group. They can ask themselves how well they accomplished their assigned task. If they admit partial or total failure, they can then ask what was left undone, and why. Also they can ask themselves how they feel toward the group. Was working with the others a satisfying or a frustrating experience? Why?

Practice in Performing Roles

It is important to gain practice in performing roles. Once group members become conscious of the roles they need to play but are not playing, each member can be asked to volunteer to play a given role during a discussion session. He is to continue to play other roles whenever he feels the urge to do so, but he is to make a special effort to see that a given function is not overlooked. If some members are habitually left out of the discussion, for example, someone can volunteer to be a *gatekeeper* or *encourager* to see that they are drawn into the group in a meaningful way. If the group too often comes up with seemingly unrelated suggestions, someone can assume the role of *coordinator* to try to relate these ideas in a practical manner. Other roles can be handled in the same way.

By using Group Leadership Role Check Sheets after each of a series of discussions, both individual members and the group as a whole can test themselves to see if they are including more and more of the functional roles and eliminating the nonfunctional ones.

Taking turns at being group observer also helps familiarize individuals with the different kinds of functional and nonfunctional roles. Perhaps at first one member should be assigned to observe the task roles, another the maintenance roles, and a third the nonfunctional roles. Still other observers can evaluate the overall operation of the group without concentrating on member roles.

Once started, the process of developing into a more mature group will provide such rewards and satisfactions that each individual's desire to maintain his membership will be enhanced. Accomplishments will bear the stamp of the total group, not of any one member. Members will recognize the superiority of group efforts over their individual attempts to do the same thing. Personal antagonisms will be minimized and differences of opinion will be valued as essential to sound group decision making. And, most important, all members will find in the activity of the group the fullest satisfaction of their basic psychological needs.

REFERENCES AND READINGS

Fiedler, F. E., & Chemers, M. M. *Leadership and effective management*. Glenview, Ill.: Scott Foresman, 1974.

Kemp, C. G. *Perspectives on the group process*. Boston: Houghton Mifflin, 1970.

Strauss, B., & Strauss, F. *New ways to better meetings*. New York: Viking Press, 1964.

Tannenbaum, R., Weschler, I., & Massarik, F. Leadership a frame of reference. In R. S. Cathcart & L. A. Samovar (Eds.), *Small group communication*. Dubuque, Iowa: Wm. C. Brown, 1970.

White, R., & Lippitt, R. Leader behavior and member reaction in three social climates. In D. Cartwright & A. Zander (Eds.), *Group dynamics: Research and theory* (3rd edition). New York: Harper & Row, 1968.

17
THE WORKSHOP FOLLOW-UP

Workshops in logical problem solving and group effectiveness are not ends in themselves, of course; they are only the beginning of the process of achieving broad citizen support for the solution of community problems.

These workshops will provide opportunities for communication between organizations and between political units within the community that have probably not taken place before. Citizens will become aware of the fact that they are not alone in their concern for certain local situations and that they have the means to bring about solutions to these problems that have a chance of gaining total community support. They will be very much aware of the strength they now possess in representing all the community-minded organizations of the area. Before the workshop evaluation session is over they will begin to ask, "Where do we go from here?"

The next step, then, is to get the participants of both the midweek and the weekend workshops to agree on a date for a two-hour evening problem-identification workshop.

THE PROBLEM-IDENTIFICATION WORKSHOP

Again the optimum number of participants for such a workshop is thirty, but up to sixty can take part, as most of the work will be done in small groups. As before, tables will be required for the separate groups, there should be blank wall spaces (or easels) on which newsprint can be hung at the end of the tables, and it will be desirable to have seating for all the participants in joint sessions.

When the workshop members have assembled and have numbered off for the groups they are to work in, they should be instructed to list all the community problems that they think they can do something about. They should be cautioned not to get involved in discussing the "whys and wherefores" of the problems, but simply to write them on the newsprint. Each group should pick its own facilitator.

While the small groups are in session the coordinator should move unobtrusively among the groups and see that they are operating according to the procedures they learned in their basic workshops, recognizing that for some it will be all too easy to fall back into old, inefficient procedures.

For some groups it may take an hour or more to come up with a reasonably complete list of community problems. Since different reports are to be combined, it will not be necessary for each group to produce an exhaustive list. When the moderator feels that the groups have done an adequate job, he should call them together in joint session and ask the facilitators to hang their sheets of newsprint where they can be read by all.

If one list seems most complete, he can ask the facilitator for that group to read off the problems and then ask the other facilitators to add any problems from their own lists that have not already been mentioned. In some cases the same problem may be worded in different ways, and the coordinator should seek agreement on which statement is preferred. Occasionally he will find that what seems to be one problem is actually two different ones, and restatements will be needed.

The coordinator should ask some member of the workshop to write on another sheet of newsprint hung alongside the rest the consolidated list of problems recognized by the workshop participants. When this has been completed, the groups may go back to their separate tables to establish priorities on how the problems should be tackled. The coordinator can suggest two criteria for setting priorities: (1) that a problem is so pressing that the group members feel they cannot move on to other things until it is taken care of or (2) that the problem appears to be one they can solve fairly easily and thus gain the sense of accomplishment and confidence in achieving results that is essential to their continued operation.

When the groups have set their priorities, the coordinator should call them together in joint session to consolidate their efforts. Since it can be assumed that all those who participated in the original basic workshops will want to be involved in the problem-solving activities, and since task forces of a dozen or more people should be adequate for most problems, different groups can be organized to work on several problems at the same time. A separate sheet should be set up for each problem and the members present encouraged to sign whichever one they want to work on. Then the members who signed up for each problem should select a temporary chairman and agree upon a time and place to hold their first meeting.

Preliminary Organization of the Task Forces

Before the evening is over the coordinator should call the participants back into a final joint session to suggest the procedures to follow when they begin working as separate task forces. These should include:

1. choosing a chairman whose job will be to keep the coordinator informed of whatever decisions their task force makes so that he can pass on this information to the various organizations represented, and, where desirable, see that it is publicized in the local newspapers;

2. doing as much of their work in small groups as possible to maximize individual involvement;

3. following the steps in the problem-solving process, making sure to include those people in the community who have a special contribution to make, and asking these individuals to remain as members of the task force if it seems useful. (While these individuals have not benefited from the training in group procedures and may cause some difficulties at first, they will learn from the experience of working with those who have been trained—if the latter have the courage and the determination to do the job right.)

It will be up to the coordinator to see that all who participated in the original basic workshops are informed by letter of the evening's decisions. He should list the problems agreed upon and those for which task forces are being organized. He should give the name and address of the temporary chairman and the time and place of the first meeting of each group. And he should encourage those who did not attend the problem-identification workshop to indicate by letter or telephone which of the task forces they wish to work with.

The coordinator should also see that the work of the various task forces is made known to the city, county, and regional agencies that have a special concern for those problems. Planning commissions, for example, which are working on the same problems, can be an excellent source of data and can offer alternative choices. Most planning commissions are aware that the governmental units that must approve their planning recommendations will more readily agree to implement these plans if they have broad community support.

Final Report Session

When each task force has come up with a set of recommendations, a joint meeting should be called for task force members, the officers of their respective organizations, representatives of public and private agencies that have a stake in the particular problem areas, members of the various political bodies in the area, and local officials. Members of the press should be invited to this meeting and copies of the reports should be given to them so that the local papers can accurately cover the task-force findings.

Each chairman of the different task forces should be called on to report on his group's recommendations. After each report, comments and questions should be solicited. If members of the audience have constructive suggestions to make, the members of the relevant task force should have the privilege of accepting or not accepting them, unless there is a very strong expression of the audience's wishes.

For their recommendations, the various task forces should have solicited the support of the community organizations they represent. An indication of this support should be included in the reports. If this has not been done, then the officers of the community-minded organizations present at this meeting should be asked to put the combined task-force recommendations before their organizations for formal approval.

The Ad Hoc Nature of the Task Forces

If the task forces have completed their recommendations and have submitted their reports at this final session, they can consider their job done. Some will be inspired by the experience to want to regroup and undertake the solution of other problems on the original list.

At this point the coordinators should see that these new problem-solving ventures are not undertaken by splinter groups, but, insofar as possible, by a community-wide consolidated effort. In order to bring this about, a second problem-identification session can be called at which the original list of problems can be updated, new priorities can be established, and new task forces organized to deal with them.

THE COMMUNITY FORUM

There is another approach to community problems that contrasts with the ad hoc manner that has been repeatedly recommended here.

Community leaders who have been involved in problem-solving workshops realize that a great deal of factual information is needed just to stimulate awareness that there are problems. They also recognize that the community may differ strongly over possible solutions because of conflicting interests, inadequate or distorted information, failure to see the problem in its broader context, and unwillingness to accept the idea that compromise is an essential element in true democracy.

The Arlington Committee of 100

A community forum is one way to bring before the community the information it needs to begin to tackle its problems. It is a way to air and test conflicting points of view. A model for such a forum that has been in operation for many years (and has been copied successfully in other communities) is the Arlington Committee of 100 of Arlington, Virginia.[1]

During and after World War II, Arlington, a northern Virginia county that is a part of metropolitan Washington, D.C., was faced with many problems due to the influx of outsiders holding jobs in Washington who found the Virginia side of the Potomac the ideal place to live. Faced with increasing enmity, bitterness, and disharmony in community affairs, a group of public-spirited citizens who represented various points of view organized the Committee of 100 to provide an open forum for the discussion of all kinds of public issues.

The Committee made it a rule never to pass resolutions on public issues nor to make recommendations to legislative bodies. However, as individuals, the members of the Committee have had considerable influence in the development of public policy in the area. Many major innovations in local public policy during the past two decades were first discussed in the Committee's meetings.

The Committee fosters the study and discussion of a wide variety of existing and emerging problems—economic, cultural, governmental, social, educational, even religious. By serving as a sounding board for important policy ideas when they are being formed, the Committee contributes significantly to developing community goals. Through its educational methods, it opens closed minds, facilitates needed policy innovations in local government and other community institutions, and softens resistance to needed change.

The membership of the Committee of 100 (which now exceeds 200 families) is drawn equally from the business and the purely residential populations of the county. The Committee is made up of those who have demonstrated a vital interest in the development of the county by their past participation in civic affairs. New members are nominated

---

[1] "The Organization Every Community Needs," in *How to Get Things Changed* (New York: Doubleday, 1974) by Bert Strauss and Mary E. Stowe describes in interesting detail the organization of the Loudoun Committee of 55 in Loudoun County, Virginia which is similar to the older Arlington Committee of 100.

by present members and membership is conferred by the Executive Committee, which is made up of the officers and nine other members elected at an annual business meeting.

For the monthly programs the executive committee decides on the topics to be discussed, how they will be presented, and how opposing points of view can be handled. After the formal presentations, the members of the audience, who are seated in groups of six or eight at round tables, have an opportunity to discuss relevant points and to agree on questions they want to ask the speakers in the open discussion that follows.

As indicated before, the Committee of 100 does not endorse one point of view, no matter how unanimous the membership may be. The members, who usually represent the leadership of one or more civic organizations, are free to take back to these organizations whatever conclusions they have come to on the issues discussed. It is largely through these other organizations that further action takes place.

The Committee of 100 meets at dinners preceded by a social hour. When people chat over refreshments or sit down to dinner together, they get to know each other as human beings and begin to understand more fully the other person's point of view.

A civic forum, following the pattern of the Arlington Committee of 100 but tailored in size and scope to local conditions, could serve as a basis for community education of the highest caliber in cities or rural counties. It should, of course, be a volunteer undertaking by the leaders of the respective communities. The initiative to organize it could come from those who have participated in workshops in group effectiveness and logical problem solving. If professional change agents are alert, they will recognize in such a forum the many useful opportunities they have to assist in the process of planned change.

REFERENCES AND READINGS

McCluskey, H. Y. A dynamic approach to participation in community development. *Journal of the Community Development Society*, 1970, Vol. 1, No. 1, 25-32.

Strauss, B., & Stowe, M. E. *How to get things changed*. Garden City, N.Y.: Doubleday, 1974.

Swanson, B. E. *Community leadership and decision making*. Iowa City, Iowa: University of Iowa, Bulletin No. 842, 48-57.

CONCLUSION

In an age when science has provided us with so many ways of solving our technological and social problems, the process of planned change ought to smoothly and efficiently provide us with an ideal physical and social environment. Obviously this is not the case. Human nature does not yield easily to scientific method. While the majority of Americans may be in general agreement as to the kind of world they want to live in, there will always be some who, through ignorance, selfishness, or just plain hunger for power, will subordinate the common good to their own ends.

Furthermore, the idea of planned change in itself is anathema to many Americans. It suggests totalitarianism either of the left or of the right. However, since change is a constant in modern technological society, the result of failing to plan is chaos and blight in our cities and even in the open country.

The difference between planned change of the totalitarian variety and planned change in a democracy is the amount of citizen involvement in the planning process. At one extreme all planning is performed by government bureaucrats, without even token citizen participation; at the other extreme the planning is done primarily by citizens with the representatives of government agencies acting as resource persons or process stimulators.

Those who are interested in what can happen when planned change of the totalitarian variety takes place will find it profitable to follow up on this point in Hedrick Smith's informative study *The Russians (1976)*. The author makes it clear that with ample natural resources, trained manpower, and ready access to technological know-how, the bureaucratically dominated society created by the Communist party has proven so inefficient and wasteful that only a relatively small proportion of party elite enjoy amenities of life comparable to those enjoyed by most American citizens. The rest of the people not only live in physical discomfort by our standards, but are also deprived of freedom of movement, of thought, and of expression, and fear is a constant in their everyday lives.

So long as planned change is citizen oriented, the ideals of a democratic society can be maintained. When citizens participate in identifying the problems to be dealt with and in weighing alternative solutions, planned change will be in the interests of the total community.

It is not technical knowledge that counts most, but the process by which people are involved in public decision making. The professional and nonprofessional change agents who try to substitute technical know-how for a concern with the process of citizen involvement will invariably create more problems than they solve and end up maintaining a bureaucracy or agency that does not accomplish what it was created to accomplish.

What most people lack for productive participation in public decision making are the skills and understanding that make working together both creative and psychologically satisfying. Here is where the change agent, through a careful application of the material in this book and a little practice, has his unique opportunity to foster change.

REFERENCES AND READINGS

Smith, H. *The Russians*. New York: Quadrangle, 1976.

APPENDIX I:
CHANGE EFFORTS
AMONG LOW-INCOME BLACKS

Low-income blacks who live in the South or who have migrated to cities from the rural South constitute the largest distinct group of disadvantaged in America. Their high visibility in a society dominated by whites, rather than any lack of capabilities, has stood in the way of their breaking free of restraints that have held them down for generations. Yet in addition they have certain persistent group characteristics that have greatly hampered their achieving satisfactory goals on their own initiative.

We must not be led astray by the great gains that have been achieved nationally by and for blacks during the civil rights movement. These could not have been accomplished without the general prosperity, technological advances, and mobility of the American people during and following World War II. Moreover, the conscience of the majority culture was ripe for change and stimulated active support for blacks in the various branches of government, particularly the Supreme Court, as well as among church leaders and citizens generally. Had the struggle been "black versus white" only, the result might have been a standoff, not the revolutionary change that has taken place in a generation.

In common with economically disadvantaged whites in both urban and rural settings, low-income blacks have suffered from a lack of active involvement in formal group activities outside the family. They lack sophistication and experience in working together for common goals. As a consequence, in their group activities they have frequently allowed themselves to be dominated by certain institutional leaders—ministers, educators, politicians, and professional workers from government agencies. These leaders have been torn between concern for their fellow blacks and for their own status, acceptance, and promotion in the white-dominated institutions that employed them. Too often they have allowed the scales to be tipped in favor of the latter.

Many of these traditional leaders have had special knowledge or training superior to that possessed by the other blacks in the groups they served. But they have not demonstrated the know-how required for effective leadership in matters of broad, general concern. For that reason, their domination of group decision making has limited the range and effectiveness of group objectives and stifled innovative solutions to group problems and growth in group maturity.

In addition, to further their institutional, if not their personal, objectives, these leaders have tended to overemphasize the importance of status in group activities, favoring a few co-workers and diminishing the rest of the group's sense of its own adequacy. Consequently, the ability of such black groups to use all their resources to meet the needs of members has been thwarted.

Finally, low-income black neighborhood communities, far more than even the poorest white communities, have been pressured to subordinate their decision making to the will of others—local politicians and officials, employers, landlords, merchants, and sometimes just plain fellow citizens who manipulated the lives of people they could dominate with impunity. Some of these pressures were exerted directly. More often they were manifested through the traditional leaders—the ministers, educators, county agents, and others employed by government agencies. When these indirect influences were brought to bear on them it was often difficult for ordinary blacks to know whether community goals were for their own or somebody else's benefit, and their support was less than wholehearted.

While many of these adverse conditions are being corrected, they will not be fully eliminated until low-income blacks have been trained to work together effectively in formal group activities. What the average low-income black needs most is confidence in the ability of his local black community to cooperate in its own best interest, particularly in harmony with the larger community.

During and since the civil rights movement, younger and more articulate blacks have come to the fore in many Southern communities and in Northern urban neighborhoods. Many of them have been in the armed forces or have worked where they were exposed to conditions more favorable to their race than those they had grown up in. Few have seen any reason to return to being second-class citizens. They have challenged the restraints that traditional black leaders were willing to put up with. However, many of their fellows have long since made their individual adjustments to a subordinate role in society and have not always enthusiastically accepted the programs these new young leaders have offered. They have seen serious risks involved. So splinter groups have developed which have further weakened the ability of the black communities to meet even their most pressing needs.

One factor that has generally worked against these aggressive new leaders is their tendency to operate in an authoritarian manner. Unless this authoritarianism is offset by a high degree of charisma, such goals as they are able to accomplish with their fellow blacks have often proved to be short-range ones of little lasting value and not without adverse effects on the relationship between the black neighborhoods and the surrounding white community.

The tendency of both traditional black leaders and young rebels to slip into authoritarian patterns of organization has greatly hampered the achievement of group-oriented objectives. In authoritarian groups generally, building and maintaining a power structure almost invariably becomes more important than meeting member needs. Authoritarian leaders create conditions that inevitably give rise to factions that challenge their authority and split the membership of the group. Financial and other outside support for black organizations too frequently has strengthened the power of incumbent authoritarian leaders, institutionalized their relationships with their fellow members, and removed them further from the needs and wishes of their followers.

When community organizations, with public funds to improve conditions for low-income black families, have attempted to involve black representatives in their planning deliberations (often with reluctance, and primarily to meet requirements set by the Federal government) the results frequently have been unsatisfactory largely because those chosen to represent the blacks have come from one of the following categories.

1. They are acceptable primarily to the white majority and are not always seen as truly representative by their fellow blacks. Many are the so-called traditional or institutional leaders. The black groups do not feel that, through them, they are sharing in decision making, and the resulting programs fail to receive their wholehearted support.
2. Due to inadequate training and experience in group activities, they are less than articulate in expressing their feelings about proposals made in the decision-making group. Their "tongue-tied" reaction often leaves the erroneous impression that they are in agreement with the rest of the group and prevents them from making any significant contributions.

3. They are immature in their estimation of the role they are asked to play on the task force. They consider that it is their job to act as the final and unquestioned authority on all matters having to do with either blacks or the hard-core poor. They feel it is their prerogative, if not their duty, to castigate the members of the white community for past shortcomings in their dealings with minority groups. They convey the impression that those present on task forces are personally responsible for such shortcomings, when, as a matter of fact, their presence testifies to their desire to correct past injustices. Many members of the white community, whose participation and support for the program at hand is crucial, come to the unhappy conclusion that it is a waste of time to get involved in fruitless and recriminating discussions, and they drop out of the program, a consequence of disastrous proportions in some communities.

In getting such programs organized two recommendations should prove helpful. The first is that getting the facts straight is essential when the various exploratory committees are being set up to identify the needs of the low-income families in the community. In most communities there will generally be individuals, both black and white, whose work has brought them in close touch with, and made them fully accepted by, the poor. They often have a better grasp of the facts and can verbalize them more clearly than the members of the disadvantaged groups themselves. If they also know how to participate democratically in group discussions, they can serve as resource persons in the exploratory stages to provide the required information so that the organization can identify and define its problems at the start. Whether they continue to participate will be up to them and the organization in the next phase of its problem solving.

In the meantime it should be recognized that individual low-income blacks, more than anything else, need training in the skills and understandings of group effectiveness if they are to overcome the handicaps they have inherited and their lack of experience in formal group activities. If middle-class citizens with long experience in organizations can profit from such training, they, with their limited involvement, can benefit from it even more. Having undergone such training and having a better understanding of what it means to be a good group member they are in a better position to choose those best qualified to represent them on various task forces. When these steps have been followed, low-income blacks can begin to feel that they are a real part of the community program, participate intelligently and maturely when invited to do so, and give the resulting program their ongoing support.

Experience with the training of such black groups in the poverty program and with a two-year project in the Washington metropolitan area[1] funded by the Higher Education Act of 1965 has shown that low-income blacks respond very readily to such training when, in both theory and practice, it is built around the need to insure that all group members satisfy their basic psychological needs in their group activities.

People of any race who have benefited from having been raised by mature, loving, and thoughtful parents often find it difficult to recognize the existence of deep-seated needs for affection, security, and recognition. But a comparatively large proportion of low-income blacks come from broken homes or from situations where a family, in any real sense, never did exist and, therefore, they have been deprived of the satisfaction of their psychological needs from the start. Others, who were more fortunate in their family relationships, learned what it meant to be deprived of the satisfaction of these needs when they were thrown into contact with people of the majority culture in school and on the job.

From day to day these people hunger for a warm response from others, for a sense of being just as much a part of the group as anyone else, and for occasional recognition that they are contributing something of value to the group.

Low-income blacks, therefore, have little trouble knowing what group trainers are talking about when they stress the importance of the satisfaction of psychological needs in group activities. They not only know what these needs are, they feel them keenly.

This was well illustrated in a training program sponsored by a small, city-owned, Negro college in the environs of Philadelphia. Most of the groups being trained were made up of black community-action leaders, but one workshop was set up primarily for relatively young indigenous blacks who had been hired to help hard-core poor black families adopt desirable new practices in their homes and in their personal habits. These young people, who rarely had a high school education, had previously been exposed to training that was supposedly geared to their particular needs by a group of educators from a nearby university. This training program had been hastily thrown together to qualify for Federal funding. Whatever merits it may have had, it did not help these young blacks solve the face-to-face people

---

[1]See *Community Education: An Approach to Urban Problems* by Donald R. Fessler, Lyle Bryant, and Bert Strauss. Blacksburg, Virginia, Cooperative Extension Service, Circular 1059, 1968 (a report of the Northern Virginia Pilot Project in Community Education).

problems with which they were expected to deal every day, and most of them had built up a resistance to further training as a result.

But after the program got under way, they became involved at the very start in satisfying their own psychological needs in the workshop itself, and then, when they were shown why these procedures worked, they began to see how the insights could solve some of their on-the-job problems, and they relaxed and participated with obvious enthusiasm. In the other workshops in the Philadelphia area the same reaction was evident among the black community leaders who had been faced with apathy, indifference, poor attendance, and poor support for organization goals on the part of the lower-income blacks in their respective neighborhoods—the very people they knew must be involved if their community action programs were to serve the purposes for which they were intended. From their workshop experience these black leaders acquired skills and understandings that they could readily see would help them draw more of the disadvantaged blacks into their group activities, and they were deeply appreciative.

In various parts of the United States there are sizeable ethnic groups that suffer from some of the same handicaps found among low-income blacks. They have physical characteristics (not color alone) that distinguish them from members of the majority culture and/or language problems that tend to hamper communication with their white neighbors and further limit their chances of gainful employment. Some also have religious affiliations that make them objects of distrust.

These minority groups include the Puerto Ricans, Mexican-Americans, American Indians, and Orientals. Like low-income blacks, most of these people have had limited experience in formal group activities and have been encouraged to remain in a relationship of almost child-like dependence upon their institutional leaders. As a result few of them are in a position at the start to participate intelligently or effectively in democratically-oriented groups.

The procedures for preparing them for involvement in change efforts should follow along the same lines recommended for blacks and the disadvantaged in general. Those who have language problems need special consideration. They should receive their group training from individuals who not only have a mastery of their language, but have a thorough understanding of the culture from which they come. Communication is not just a matter of words; but involves basic concepts and values which differ from culture to culture.

APPENDIX II: GROUP LEADERSHIP ROLE CHECK SHEET

	Roles Played by Others	Roles That I Played
Task Roles		
Initiating	⸻	⸻
Information or Opinion Seeking	⸻	⸻
Information or Opinion Giving	⸻	⸻
Clarifying or Elaborating	⸻	⸻
Coordinating	⸻	⸻
Summarizing	⸻	⸻
Consensus Testing	⸻	⸻
Testing Feasibility	⸻	⸻
Group Maintenance Roles		
Encouraging	⸻	⸻
Expressing Group Feeling	⸻	⸻
Harmonizing	⸻	⸻
Compromising	⸻	⸻
Gate Keeping	⸻	⸻
Standard Setting	⸻	⸻
Consensus Testing	⸻	⸻
Following	⸻	⸻
Nonfunctional Roles		
Being Aggressive	⸻	⸻
Blocking	⸻	⸻
Recognition Seeking	⸻	⸻
Being a Playboy	⸻	⸻
Dominating	⸻	⸻
Help Seeking	⸻	⸻
Special Interest Pleading	⸻	⸻

APPENDIX III:
DEVELOPING LISTENING SKILLS

Individuals who have long played leader roles in various organizational activities usually have difficulty becoming effective group facilitators. They have not learned to listen to what others have to say and need help in overcoming their tendency to dominate the discussion.

One procedure that has been found helpful during workshops in group effectiveness is to have each group member sit through a small-group session as a group process observer. Each member in turn sits outside the group and is given a sociogram (see following page) on which he is instructed to show how often each member of the group participates in the discussion. First, the observer identifies each circle on the sociogram with a member of the group, putting an X through the circle or circles that are in excess of the number in the group. When the discussion begins, he puts his pencil on the circle representing the person who is speaking. As soon as anyone else speaks, he draws a line to the circle representing that person and holds it there until a third speaks, and so on. He need not bother putting in arrows to show the direction of the discussion. Regardless of how interesting the discussion may become to him personally, he is forbidden to participate as long as he is the observer.

The sociograms for all the groups can be numbered by group and session and posted together so that the workshop participants can see during the course of the workshop whether or not there are any changes in the amount of individual participation in their group discussions and whether or not their facilitators facilitated or led.

If each small discussion group selects a new observer at the beginning of each small-group discussion, that person can become the facilitator at the following session and will be better prepared to listen to others. Sociograms will need to be prepared ahead of time for use in workshop sessions.

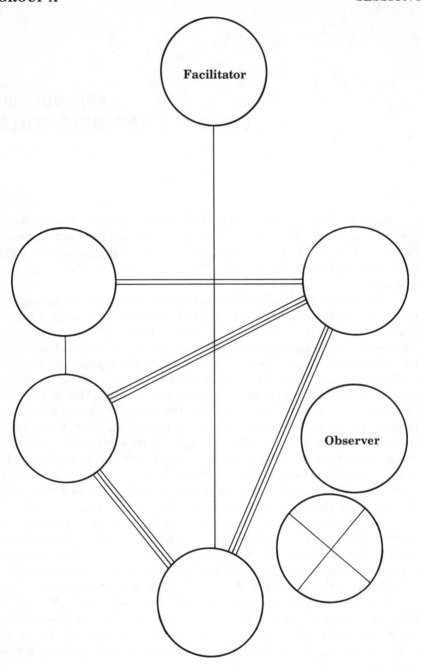